Biblical Sinai traditions

Israel Knohl

Biblical Sinai traditions

Israel Knohl
The Hebrew University
Jerusalem, Israel

ISBN 978-3-031-77982-4   ISBN 978-3-031-77983-1   (eBook)
https://doi.org/10.1007/978-3-031-77983-1

This Palgrave Macmillan imprint is published by the registered company Springer Nature Switzerland AG.
The registered company address is: Gewerbestrasse 11, 6330 Cham, Switzerland

If disposing of this product, please recycle the paper.

Contents

CHAPTER 1

Foreword

The leading voice in the Hebrew Bible is the familiar voice of the Biblical narrative. According to this narrative in Exodus and Deuteronomy, Mt. Sinai, or "Horeb" is the location of the most important event in the history of Ancient Israel and its beliefs. It is on this mountain that God revealed Himself to all of Israel, and it is there that the nation heard the Ten Commandments given by God. It is on this mountain that Moses received the additional Torah Laws to be transmitted to Israel. And it is in the context of this revelation at Sinai-Horeb that a covenant was created between the nation and its God. The nation then breached the covenant by creating the Golden Calf. In response, Moses shattered the Tablets of the Covenant, the stone tablets containing the Ten Commandments (Exodus 19-39, Deuteronomy 5: 2-30, 8-21).

However, besides this narrative, the Bible hides another voice that was silenced by the dominant tradition over the course of the years. In this version, those foundational events occurred in a completely different way: the nation heard the Ten Commandments not at Mt. Sinai, but beside a spring; the covenant and its breach also took place beside that same spring; and the Divine revelation next to the spring was egalitarian, without an intermediary: neither Moses, nor any other person. From this perspective, Mt. Sinai was not the place where God gave the Ten Commandments to the nation, but rather the place from which God began His march to the place of revelation.

© The Author(s), under exclusive license to Springer Nature Switzerland AG 2024
I. Knohl, *Biblical Sinai traditions*,
https://doi.org/10.1007/978-3-031-77983-1_1

This conflicting tradition is hidden among the verses of ancient Biblical poetry—poetry that was composed many years before the leading narrative. How, when, and why was the alternative tradition silenced? Who silenced it and what interest did they have in doing so? What are the ideological and spiritual meanings concealed in the silenced tradition? And what did the original narrator of the Sinai narrative seek to innovate by moving the location of the revelation from the spring to the mountain?

The northern narrator's adaptation and reediting of the ancient poetic materials on the Sinaitic tradition and the revelation at the spring is an early and masterful example of creative inner biblical interpretation. In his bold interpretative course, the northern author moved the focal point of the verbal revelation from the peaceful spring to the volcanic and thunderous mountain, Sinai—Horeb. By doing this, the narrator created an essential arena for Moses as the mediator of revelation. Furthermore, this shift opened the door to the scene of an intimate and secret revelation of God to Moses, the contents of which will only be revealed to the people of Israel much later. Over the generations, many authors and scribes entered through this opening, and they expanded the contents of the Sinaitic revelation: the writers of Deuteronomy, the authors of the Book of Jubilees,[1] the Sages, the Kabbalists.

The creative interpretation of the northern narrator turned biblical religion into a religion of prophetic revelation centered on Moses, the father of the prophets.[2]

BIBLIOGRAPHY

H. Najman, 2009, *Seconding Sinai*, Atlanta.

B.D. Sommer, 2015, *Revelation and Authority: Sinai in Jewish Scripture and Tradition* (The Anchor Yale Bible Reference Library), New Haven CT.

---

[1] See, Najman (2009).

[2] Benjamin David Sommer's recently published book, "Revelation and Authority: Sinai in Jewish Scripture and Tradition" (Sommer 2015), is a rich and important study of the various traditions regarding the Revelation at Sinai in the Torah, and the ways they were understood and explained in post-Scripture Judaism. However, the focus of Sommer's work differs from the focus of this work. He focuses on the theological aspects of the character and nature of the Divine Revelation at Sinai, while I discuss the literary-historical aspects of the development of traditions regarding the transmission of the Laws and the Covenant in the desert in light of the cultural and social changes in Israel during the Biblical era.

CHAPTER 2

The Beginning of Writing and the Beginning of Biblical Literature

The question of the prevalence of literacy in ancient Israel must be the point of departure for any investigation of the genesis of the traditions regarding the covenant between Israel and its God, and the giving of the Torah and the Laws in the desert. In other words, we must clarify at what point Israel became "the People of the Book", and when and how it developed the material and spiritual infrastructure necessary for the writing of Biblical traditions. It is in this way that we will be able to peer through the veil of this early stage to the days preceding the development of literacy in Israel. We will then be able to get to know the character of the ancient compositions composed when only a few people knew how to read and write.

Evidence from the Hebrew Bible alone cannot answer these questions. We must turn to archeological findings and Israel's neighboring cultures during the Biblical era. These will enrich our sources and establish the discussion on a relatively firm foundation.

The picture that arises from Egyptian and Mesopotamian cultures indicate that literacy was the domain of the elite educated class in the temples and royal courts. This is consistent with the characteristics of the languages and scripts of these cultures, Akkadian and Egyptian, which contain thousands of symbols with sometimes more than one meaning or use. Naturally,

I. Knohl, *Biblical Sinai traditions*, https://doi.org/10.1007/978-3-031-77983-1_2

3

literacy was not widespread among commoners in this environment.[1] The development of the alphabet, which occurred either in Egypt or the Sinai Desert around the eighteenth century BC, made things somewhat simpler. Limiting written symbols to a few dozen letters made learning to read and write easier.[2]

Despite the alphabetic revolution, the spread of literacy was evidently slow.[3] This is apparent from archaeological evidence from Israel. Very few Hebrew inscriptions have been found from the period before the eighth century BC. Meaning the use of writing to pass on messages and spread knowledge, whether economic, administrative, or spiritual, was very minimal and was apparently limited to the educated elite classes among the priests and in royal courts.[4]

As mentioned above, it appears that the turning point for the dissemination of literacy began at about 800 BC. The first indications of the expansion of writing were discovered in the Kingdom of Israel. A collection of ostraca, termed the Samaria Ostraca, was discovered in the kingdom's capital and has been dated to the first half of the eighth century BC. The distinct increase of the distribution of epigraphic findings,

---

[1] For more on scribal culture and the frameworks in which scribes wrote, see for instance van der Toorn (2007), 51–108.

[2] Scholars are divided on question of the place in which the alphabet developed: whether it was Egypt, Sinai, or Canaan. For the various opinions see Goldwasser (2015, 2022), and for another perspective see, Sass (1991); Darnell et al. (2005, 73–91). Though interesting in its own right, this problem is not relevant to the issue being discussed here- the development of literacy and literary creation in Israel during the first millennium BC.

[3] For a critical evaluation of the alphabetic period and its accessibility: Warner (1980).

[4] The position expressed here is similar to a position that has been coined "socio-archaeological"; that is to say, one that investigates that historical question of the rate of literacy in Israel and Judah during the Biblica period through material finds and uses those finds as well as sociological evidence for analysis. Biblical texts are compared to the picture that arises from material findings from this period. The primary articulation of this approach towards literacy can be found in Jamieson-Drake (1991). This approach has mostly been accepted— with a few changes and some variety. A clear and prominent representation of this in Israeli scholarship can be found in the works of Nadav Na'aman, such as Na'aman (2002, 13ff). See also: Rollston (2010); Rollston (2018); Finkelstein and Sass (2013); Finkelstein (2020). For the recent application of this approach on the development of the Biblical text, see for instance, Finkelstein and Silberman (2001); Finkelstein and Silberman (2006); Knauf (2002); Schniedewind (2004); Schmid (2012). For a critical evaluation of this approach see for instance, van der Toorn, ibid., 3, as well as Emerton (2006); Richelle (2016). An updated survey of research on the subject of literacy was recently presented by Burlingame (2019).

especially material that is not administrative but literary, is noticeable during this period both within the borders of the Kingdom of Israel as well as in areas under its influence.[5]

In Judah, the trend began about fifty years later. From the start of the second half of the eighth century, there are more indications that the use of reading and writing, (such as the Siloam inscription and the administrative "for the king" impressions), was wider spread.

An additional sign of the cultural changes of this period in Israel is reflected in the Biblical collection. The course of the eighth century BC marked the appearance of "the literal prophets". In contrast to previous prophets and miracle workers such as Elijah and Elisha, that nobody wrote down their prophecies, now we have the written prophecies of four seers who were active during this time period: first, Amos and Hosea ben Beeri, who prophesied in the Kingdom of Israel. Then, Isaiah ben Amoz, and Micah of Morasheth-Gat who were active in Judah during the reign of Hezekiah King of Judah. As already noted in the Talmud notes, these four prophets who prophesized during this same period.[6] The place and order of appearance of the four prophets is congruent with our knowledge from archaeological findings. The Kingdom of Israel, where Amos was active during the second quarter of the eighth century BC, during the days of Jeroboam II ben Jehoash, is first. After him came Hosea, who prophesized during the years 750–725 BC. Finally, Isaiah and Micah were active toward the end of the eighth century BC, in the Kingdom of Judah.

The expansion of literacy and its growing popularity is also reflected in the content of these prophets' visions. Isaiah is commanded to write down his prophecies (see, Isaiah 8:1). It's possible that he himself wrote down all his prophecies, or it is possible that he wrote down some of his prophecies himself and others were transcribed by his students.[7] In any case, as soon as prophecies were written down they could be distributed to the public and passed on to future generations- even if at the outset they were preserved within the small circle of the prophet's loyal servants. In addition, as soon as the number of readers in Israel grew, people were able

[5] Such as, "The Book of Balaam" from Deir Alla, and a piece of poetry from Kuntillet Ajrud. See also, Ahituv, Inscriptions, 262–266, 405–427.
[6] Talmud B. Bava Batra 14.
[7] It is possible that this is the meaning of, "seal the instructions with My disciples", Isaiah 8:16.

to read the prophecy and disseminate the prophet's messages to those who could not read.[8]

The sharp cultural turn in Israel and Judah during this time is apparent in the comparison between the first writing prophets and their predecessors, Elijah and Elisha, who were active about a century prior in the Kingdom of Israel. They represent a different cultural experience. It is fair to assume that they also prophesized. Fragments of their prophecies have even survived in the stories about them in the Book of Kings.[9] And yet, we do not have any books of prophecies authored by them. Almost the only thing left of them are the stories of their wonders. However, these stories themselves attest that they occurred and were handed down verbally and not in writing, nor in an especially educated environment (Kings II 8:4). It is even possible that Elijah and Elisha themselves were illiterate. One way or another, it is doubtful that there was a high rate of literacy in Israel of the ninth century, during which these prophets were active. Clearly, there was no real reason to write down large works, whether to distribute them or to transmit them to future generations, given the non-negligible material cost and the audience.

And so, the eighth century BC is the watershed line. Before then only a few people were literate in Israel. But over the course of the next century, and after it, Israel became "the People of the Book". Messages and ideas were transmitted and preserved in writing. This cultural turning point was not limited to the technical field alone. As mentioned, and as I will discuss in more detail below, up until then literacy had been limited to the ruling classes or the elite circles close to it. When literacy expanded, other classes also wrote down their creations. And with this, some of the voices of the opposition, such as the admonitions of those four prophets to the rulers and social elite, is revealed to us.

At the same time, as hinted previously, this conclusion is not robust enough to negate the possibility that writing existed in a limited scope in

---

[8] On the appearance of the "Prophets of the Book" see, most recently: Millard (2010) (he also refers to the passages from the Isaiah, mentioned above, there), as well as Nissinen (2014). For insight into the technical terms for writing in Isaiah 8:1 see Williamson (2011).

[9] This is especially apparent in the political-military context. Just like the writing prophets (cf. Isaiah 7:3–9, for instance), their predecessors were also involved in the political and military sphere- as prophets of encouragement and support (see, for instance, Kings II 3:16–19, 13:14–19) or as a source of authority and Divine power (Kings II, 8:7–16).

the centers of power and religion before the eighth century. It seems that ritual teachings for priests were written down in the central temples.[10] Our knowledge of Mesopotamia and Egypt indicate that priestly writing was created by experts for experts. From the outset these documents were meant for a small circle of people with knowledge of the cult. They were not meant for a broader audience.[11] In terms of content, the priestly code in the Torah is closest to the rituals that were prevalent in Anatolia and northern Syria before the collapse of the Hittite Empire in the twelfth century B.C.[12] In addition, the literary structure of the priestly teachings is most similar to that of Hittite priestly teachings[13] in that they contain set opening and closing phrases such as "this is the rule of", "this is the rule"[14] I do not want to get into the complex question of how and when ritual knowledge spread from Anatolia and northern Syria to Canaan.[15] However, in light of the ancient roots of its type of literature, it is certainly possible that it was written down for priests in the central Temples before literacy expanded to the common people.

Early near eastern literature indicates that the royal courts also contained a space for diplomacy and wisdom where advisors and scribes were active. If so, it is possible that certain parts of the Book of Proverbs, Wisdom Literature, may have been written before the eighth century BCE.[16] It is also possible that that the remark regarding proverbs being

---

[10] On the priestly ritual instructions (i.e., Toroth תורות) see Begrich (1935).

[11] See, Cohen (1969) followed by Haran (1981, 327ff).

[12] See, my article: Knohl (2015); as well as the insights of Yitzhaq Feder, such as Feder (2010, 2011).

[13] Fishbane (1980).

[14] See, for instance, Lev. 6:2, 7, 18; 7:1, 11, 37; 14:2, 54–57.

[15] Were they a group of early Israelites who reached northern Syria? The Jebusites who ruled Jerusalem before David were Hittite. See, Ezekiel 16, 3. This echoes, for instance, in the names of David's scribes and ministers which indicate their Hittite-Hori ethnicities (II Samuel 8, 17, 20, 25 [Seraiah, Sheva]) as well as in the names of the non-Israelite population in Jerusalem (II Samuel 24:16–23 [Araunah, Arnon], and the appearance of Uriah the Hittite among David's warriors' [II Samuel 11, 3, 23, 39]); See, Mazar (1947); Weinfeld (1990, 1992, 63). We should also mention Stephanie Daley's theory regarding worship of the Israelite god in northern Syria in light of personal and place names: Dalley (1990); for a response see Zevit (1991). On the possibility that the Biblical text was influenced by Hindu-Aryan languages, see, Rabin (1970).

[16] See, for instance, Hurowitz (2012, vol. I, p. 10ff).

copied by members Hezekiah, King of Judah's, court at the end of eighth
century BCE, refers to such early writings (Proverbs 25:1).[17]

In addition to wisdom literature, it seems that books of history and
chronologies were also composed and transmitted in the courts of the
kings of Judah and Israel. There is room to infer that these documents
were first created for administrative and economic purposes. Evidence of
the existence of these types of works before the eighth century BCE comes
from the description of Shishak's journey in I Kings 14:25–28. Apparently,
the description is based on a contemporary source, without which the
memory of the Egyptian journey (925 BCE) would have been forgotten.
The structure and style of the description resembles other chronological
accounts from the ancient east and so it appears that the description in I
Kings has a source in chronological documentation.[18]

In addition to writings of the elite educated circles before the eighth
century BCE, we must also mention oral works.[19] We have been left with
a number of examples of ancient poetry in the Hebrew Bible. The genesis
of these works of poetry was oral and they were transmitted orally through
the generations. The unique literary forms of the poetry made them easy
to memorize and transmit even without writing. In this way poetry
retained ancient traditions that were common among the people before
the spread of literacy and the outset of narrative in the eighth century
BCE. I want to emphasize that the spread of literacy and the appearance

[17] See the discussion of Schneidewind (2004), as well as the possibility raised by
H.L. Ginsberg, that these were a way of transporting proverbs from the Kingdom of Israel
(Ginsberg 1982, 37, ft. 35). On its own, the opening in Proverbs 35:1, is another possible
proof of the cultural turning point that occurred in Judah at the end of the eighth century,
when the literary operation in Hezekiah's court began.

[18] On the chronographic material now embedded in the Book of Kings, see Na'aman
(2002, 78–94), and ibid., previous literature. On the importance of the description of
Shishak's journey in the Book of Kings as evidence of the accounting of history in Israel in
the early years of the kingdom, see Na'aman, ibid., and earlier in his essay: Na'aman (1996).
On the awareness of foreign kings in the Book of Kings as a sign of the existence of ancient
contemporary sources, see, Halpern (2000). On the connection between the accounting of
history and the chronological documentation and omens in the ancient east see for instance,
Finkelstein (1963).

[19] Another perspective on the elitist writing in administrative circles and the priesthood
arises from the discovery of a substantial number of seal prints, "bullae" in the City of David.
The excavators dated them to the ninth century BCE: Reich et al. (2007). See also, the
recent discussion in Rollston (2017), who believes that literacy before the eighth century was
limited to Jerusalem and its close neighbors; meaning, the centers of power and the elite
circles that were active there and around there.

of narrative did not bring about the end of poetry. To the contrary, narratives and poetry continued to exist side by side for hundreds of years to come.[20]

BIBLIOGRAPHY

J. Begrich, 1935, "Die priestliche Torah", in P. Volz et al. (eds.), *Werden und Wesen des Alten Testaments* (BZAW 66), Berlin, 63–88.

A. Burlingame, 2019, "Writing and Literacy in the World of Ancient Israel: Recent Developments and Future Directions", *Bibliotheca Orientalis* 76, 46–74.

C. Cohen, 1969, "Was the P Document Secret?", *JANES* 112, 39–44.

J.C. Darnell, F.W. Dobbs-Allsopp, M.J. Lundberg, P.K. McCarter, B. Zuckerman and C. Manassa, 2005, "Two Early Alphabetic Inscriptions from the Wadi el-Ḥôl: New Evidence for the Origin of the Alphabet from the Western Desert of Egypt", *AASOR* 59, 64–124.

S. Dalley, 1990, "Yahweh in Hamath in the 8th Century BC: Cuneiform Material and Historical Deductions", *VT* 40, 21–32.

J.A. Emerton, 2006, "The Kingdoms of Judah and Israel and Ancient Hebrew History Writing", in: S.E. Fassberg and H. Hurvitz (eds.), *Biblical Hebrew in the Northwest Semitic Setting*, Jerusalem – Winona Lake IN, 33–49.

Y. Feder, 2010, "A Levantine Tradition: The Kizzuwatnean Blood Rite and Biblical Sin Offering", in: Y. Cohen et al. (eds.), *Pax Hethitica (Fs. I. Zinger)*, Wiesbaden, 101–114.

Y. Feder, 2011, *Blood Expiation in Hittite and Biblical Ritual: Origigns, Context and Meaning*, Atlanta GA.

Israel Finkelstein, 2020, "The Emergence and Dissemination of Writing in Judah", *Semitica et Classica* 13, 269–282.

I. Finkelstein and B. Sass, 2013, "Alphabetic Inscriptions, Late Bronze II to Iron IIA: Archeological Context , Distribution and Chronology", *HeBaI* 2, 149–220.

I. Finkelstein and N.A. Silberman, 2001, *The Bible Unearthed: Archaeology's New Vision of Ancient Israel and the Origin of Its Sacred Texts*, New York.

I. Finkelstein and N.A. Silberman, 2006, *David and Solomon: In Search of the Bible's Sacred Kings and the Roots of the Western Tradition*, New York.

Joel J. Finkelstein, 1963, "Mesopotamian Historiography", *Proceedings of the American Philosophical Society* 107, 461–472.

M. Fishbane, 1980, "Biblical Colophons, Textual Criticism and Legal Analogies", *CBQ* 42, 438–449.

H.L. Ginsberg, 1982, *The Israelian Heritage of Judaism*, New York.

---

[20] This is in contrast to Robert Kawashima's theory that the birth of narrative led to the end of poetry: Kawashima (2004, 14).

O. Goldwasser, 2015, "The Invention of the Alphabet: On 'Lost Papyri' and the Egyptian Alphabet", in: C. Rico and C. Attucci (eds.), *Origins of the Alphabet: Proceedings of the First Polis Institute Interdisciplinary Conference*, Cambridge, 124–140.

O. Goldwasser, 2022, "The Early Alphabetic Inscriptions Found by the Shrine of Hathor at Serabit el-Khadem: Palaeography, Materiality, and Agency", *IEJ* 72, 14–48.

B. Halpern, 2000, "The State of Israelite History", in: G.N. Knoppers and J.G. McConville (eds.), *Reconsidering Israel and Judah*, Winona Lake IN, 540–565.

M. Haran, 1981, "Behind the Scenes of History: Determining the Date of the Priestly Source", *JBL* 100, 321–333.

A.V. Hurowitz, 2012, *Proverbs* ((Mikra Leyisrael), vol. I–II, Tel Aviv [in Hebrew].

D.W. Jamieson-Drake, 1991, *Scribes and Schools in Monarchic Judah: A Socio-Archaeological Approach*, Sheffield.

R. S. Kawashima, 2004, *Biblical Narrative and the Death of the Rhapsode*, Bloomington IN.

E.A. Knauf, 2002, "Towards an Archaeology of the Hexateuch", in: J.C. Gertz et al. (eds.), *Abschied vom Jahwisten* (BZAW 315), Berlin, 277–294.

I. Knohl, 2015, "P and Traditions of Northern Syria and Southern Anatolia", in: F. Landy et al. (eds.), *Text, Time and Temple: Historical and Ritual Studies in Leviticus*, Sheffield, 63–69.

B. Mazar, 1947, "The Scribe of King David and the Problem of the High Officials in the Ancient Kingdom of Israel", *BJPES* 13, 105–114 [in Hebrew].

A. Millard, 2010, "'Take a Large Tablet and Write on it': Isaiah – A Writing Prophet?", in: K.J. Dell et al. (eds.), *Genesis, Isaiah and Psalms (Fs. J.A. Emerton)*, Leiden, 105–117.

N. Na'aman, 1996, "The Contribution of the Amarna Letters to the Debate on Jerusalem's Political Position in the Tenth Century B.C.E", *BASOR* 304, 17–27.

N. Na'aman, 2002, *The Past that Shapes the Present. The Creation of Biblical Historiography in the Late First Temple Period and After the Downfall* (Yeriot 3), Jerusalem.

M. Nissinen, 2014, "Since When Do Prophets Write?", in: K. de Troyer et al. (eds.), *In the Footsteps of Sherlock Holmes (Fs. A. Aejmelaus)*, Leuven, 585–606.

Rabin, 1970, ח' רבין, "מלים בעברית המקראית מלשון האינדו-ארים שבמזרח הקרוב", ש' אברמסקי ואחרים (עורכים), ספר שמואל ייבין, ירושלים, 462–497.

R. Reich, O. Lernau and E. Shukron, 2007, "Recent Discoveries in the City of David, Jerusalem", *IEJ* 57, 153–169.

M. Richelle, 2016, "Elusive Scrolls: Could Any Hebrew Literature Have Been Written Prior to the Eighth Century BCE?" *VT* 66, 556–594.

C.A. Rollston, 2010, *Writing and Literacy in the World of Ancient Israel: Epigraphic Evidence from the Iron Age*, Atlanta GA.

C.A. Rollston, 2017, "Epigraphic Evidence from Jerusalem and its Environs at the Dawn of Biblical History: Methodologies and a Long Duree Perspective", *NSJAR* XI, 7*–20*.

C.A. Rollston, 2018, "Scripture and Inscriptions: Eighth-Century Israel and Judah in Writing", in: Z.I. Farber and J.L. Wright (eds.), *Archaeology and History of Eighth-Century Judah*, Atlanta GA, 457–473.

B. Sass, 1991, "The Beth Shemesh Tablet and the Early History of the Proto-Canaanite, Cuneiform and South Semitic Alphabets", *UF* 23, 315–326.

K. Schmid, 2012, *The Old Testament: A Literary History* (eng. transl.: L.M. Malony), Minneapolis.

W.M. Schniedewind, 2004, *How the Bible Became a Book: The Textualization of Ancient Israel*, Cambridge.

K. van der Toorn, 2007, *Scribal Culture and the Making of the Hebrew Bible*, Cambridge MA – London.

S.M. Warner, 1980, "The Alphabet: An Innovation and its Diffusion", *VT* 30, 81–90.

M. Weinfeld, 1990, "Traces of Hittite Cult in Shiloh and in Jerusalem", *Shnaton* 10, 107–114 [in Hebrew].

M. Weinfeld, 1992, *From Joshua to Josiah: Turning Points in the History of Israel from the Conquest of the Land Until the Fall of Judah*, Jerusalem [in Hebrew].

H.G.M. Williamson, 2011, "The Practiaclities of Prophetic Writing in Isaiah 8:1", in: *On Stone and Scroll (Fs. G.I. Davies)* (BZAW 420), Berlin, 357–369.

Z. Zevit, 1991, "Yahweh Worship and Worshippers in 8th-century Syria", *VT* 41, 363–366.

CHAPTER 3

The Location of Mt. Sinai in Hebrew Biblical Poetry

In the chapter above we learned that the Hebrew Bible can, largely speaking, be divided into two main stages of development. The earliest stages are reflected in verses of poetry that preserve oral traditions. The narrative tradition, on the other hand, reflects a later stage of composition when literacy was widespread in Israel.

As such, the traditions regarding Mt. Sinai, the giving of the Law, and the covenant in the desert should be seen through the lens of this division. We will first explore the early poetic descriptions of these events and in doing so, sketch a portrait of ancient Israelite tradition.[1]

Many scholars agree upon the early date of Deborah's Song (Judges 5).[2] It was probably composed not long after the events described in it occurred: the war between Israel and the Kings of Canaan. The Philistines are not mentioned in the Song. They were not yet a regional power. This fits the reality of the twelfth century BCE, give or take, when the Israelite settlement was mainly confined to the mountains, and the Canaanites

---

[1] Lately there have been a number of scholars who date these poems later. Among the most prominent is Pfeiffer (2005). However, this view does not sit well with me. This theory does not explain the apparent unique concept reflected in the poems, which connects between YHWH and Mt. Sinay located in the southern area of eastern Jordan. Why these poems "swim against the tide" of Hebrew Biblical narratives that establish the location of Mt. Sinai in the area we now know as the Sinai Desert? For literature on the subject and a critical evaluation of these theories see, Leunenberger (2010, 2017).

[2] Echols (2008, 42–63).

© The Author(s), under exclusive license to Springer Nature Switzerland AG 2024
I. Knohl, *Biblical Sinai traditions*,
https://doi.org/10.1007/978-3-031-77983-1_3

controlled the Jezreel Valley, Beit Shaan Valley and the coastline. The El-Amarna documents indicate that the Canaanite regime was one of city-states. Every city controlled its close environs and was ruled by a king.[3] Similar political situation can be seen in the language of the Song: "The kings came; they fought; then fought the/ kings of Canaan, at Taanach,/ by the waters of Megiddo…" (Judges 5:19) Megiddo is located at a strategic crossroads between the plains and Jezreel Valley. Because of its critical location, it was the site of battles stretching back into ancient times. For instance, the Battle of Megiddo during the fifteenth century BCE is which is maybe the earliest description of a battle in human history: The Egyptian Pharoah, Thutmose III fought there against the Canaanites and following his victory, Egypt ruled over Canaan for the next three centuries.

At the point at which the Song of Deborah describes the war between Israel and Canaan, Egypt was no longer a regional power and the vacuum it left behind was the source of contention between Israel and the Canaanites. The poet is familiar with the small details of the day of battle. For instance, in Judges 5:23 the poet curses a small settlement not familiar to us from any different source: "Curse Meroz, says the angel of the Lord;/curse bitterly its inhabitants, /because they did not come to the help of the Lord,/to the help of the Lord against the mighty." The residents of Meroz are denounced for not coming to the aid of God. This is also a reflection of the poet's conception of war. The Israelites are being mustered for "the help of the Lord." The importance of volunteering is key to our understanding of the historical background of the Song.[4] In contrast to the monarchical Canaanite society, Israel does not have a king, and so also no tax, administration, or permanent army. The Israelite state did not yet exist, and its institutions had not yet been established including a standing professional army. Society in the time of the Judges was egalitarian, anti-monarchical, and its army was volunteer based.

This social-political structure is reflected in the Song's opening (Judges 5:2): "When locks are long in Israel, / when the people offer themselves willingly/ bless the Lord! And further, (verse 9): "My heart goes out to the commanders of Israel/ who offered themselves willingly among the

---

[3] This is the reality that is also reflected in the Book of Joshua, even though it is clear that it was composed years afterwards, certainly not before the end of the monarchy.

[4] On this motif in poetry and the different position of the editors of the poem see my article, Knohl (2023). In this essay I also note the literary and narrative structure of the original poem and its similarity to the numerical structure reflected in some Ugaritic texts. In my opinion this connection is also an indication of the antiquity of the Song.

people. /Bless the Lord." The poet praises and blesses the tribes who volunteered to fight. On the other hand, those who did not come to fight are derided. As the poet says about the Tribe of Reuben who stayed with their sheep in Jordan (Judges 5:16): "Why did you tarry among the sheepfolds, / to hear the piping for the flocks?" (See also, Numbers 31:2).

The picture that arises from the Song is very realistic and faithfully portrays life during the era of the Judges or Iron Age 1. Likewise, the language of the Song contains archaic structures known to us from Canaanite literature. These types of structures cannot be found in later works. For instance, the dual form in Judges 5:30: "'Are they/ not finding and dividing the spoil? /A woman or two for every man;" The word *raham* is a term for a woman, and hence *raham rahamāṯyim*, i.e., a woman or two as spoils for each warrior.[5] So too, "spoil of dyed stuffs for Sisera, /spoil of dyed stuffs embroidered, /two pieces of dyed work embroidered for my neck as spoil?'" *Raḥamāṯyim*, and *riqmātayim* (two pieces of work embroidered) are archaic dual forms that disappeared from Hebrew. This is more evidence of the antiquity of the Song.

The beginning of the Song addresses the rulers, whether the kings of Canaan, or others (Judges 5:3–5):

> Hear, O kings; give ear, O princes;
> to the LORD I will sing;
> I will make melody to the LORD, the God of Israel.
> 4 LORD, when you went out from Seir,
>   when you marched from the region of Edom,
> the earth trembled,
>   and the heavens poured;
>   the clouds indeed poured water.
> 5 The mountains quaked before the LORD, the One of Sinai,
>   before the LORD, the God of Israel.

The meaning of the verses is opaque. Does the poet mean to say that God left Seir and Edom to come intervene in battle? This is a definite possibility because the continuation of the poem ascribes the Israelite's victory to the combination of the Lord's might and human might, as described in the curse of Meroz: "because they did not come to the help of the

---

[5] This should be compared to the language of the Mesha Stele and its description of the city of Nebo which was slaughtered by the King of Moab (lines 16–17) "...women and maidens (*raḥamāṯ*...)".

Lord,/to the help of the Lord against the mighty." However, it is more likely that God's arrival at the beginning of the poem does not refer to His interference in battle, but rather hints at a foundational event in the history of Israel, when God appeared and marched before or toward His people.

Sinai is mentioned among the mountains that quaked before God when He marched out of Edom is Sinai (Judges 5:5): "The mountains quaked before the LORD, the One of Sinai,/ before the LORD, the God of Israel." In light of findings from related Semitic languages it is possible that "One of Sinai", *zę sínay*, should be understood as a descriptive modifier of God, that is to say, "the God of Sinai".[6] Either way, it is clear that the text establishes the location of Sinai in a specific geographic site characterized by specific geological phenomena. God arrives from Edom-Seir which is in southern modern-day Jordan. Edom has been mentioned in Egyptian writings from as early as the thirteenth century BCE. Other contemporary documents also make note of Seir, or the "lands of Seir", and it seems that the territories of Edom and Seir largely overlapped. The close connection between the territories is also reflected in the stores of the Forefathers. Esau the father of Edom (Genesis 25:30), is also a man of Seir (Genesis 36, 25; 39, 11). The combination of the two names, Seir and Edom, into one figure is an additional indication of the overlap between the two territories in southern Jordan to the east.

God's march from Sinai in Seir-Edom is accompanied by natural phenomena (Judges 5:4–5): "the earth trembled, / and the heavens poured;/ the clouds indeed poured water. /The mountains quaked before the LORD." First let's consider: "the earth trembled" and "the mountains quaked before the Lord". "Quaked" רעשה apparently refers to an earthquake, similar to the "earthquake" רעש during the days of Uzziah the King of Judah, mentioned in the opening of the Book of Amos (Amos 1:1), and Zechariah 14:5.

The "quaking" of the mountain before God, refers, apparently, to volcanic activity and molten lava.[7] These characteristics of God's arrival from the south fits what we know about Edom-Seir. Southern modern-day Jordan, which was once Biblical Edom, is located on the Syrian African rift, an area that known for volcanic activity. This area also includes some of the northern part of modern-day Saudi Arabia. And indeed, Saudi Arabi

---

[6] See for instance, a discussion of the various possibilities, Holmstedt (2014).

[7] For a description of volcanic phenomena as God arrives, see Amzallag (2014).

has a great many volcanoes. None of them are currently active, but the last historical evidence of a volcanic eruption is from 1256 CE. A volcano south of Medina, the city where Muhammad, the Prophet of Islam once lived, erupted, and the molten lava almost reached the city, twenty kilometers north.[8]

This indicates that the "Sinai" that is mentioned in the Song of Deborah, is located in the vicinity of the Syrian African rift. This is not the region that is called "Sinai" today, between the Negev and the Suez Canal. There are no volcanoes or volcanic activity in the area at all! It seems then that we must look for Sinai on the other side of the Red Sea and the Suez Canal, in modern-day southern Jordan and west- northern Saudi Arabia.

Confirmation of our conclusion comes from an additional early poem. The opening of Moses's Blessings describes God's arrival from Sinai (Deuteronomy 33:2): "The Lord came from Sinai/and dawned from Seir upon us;/ he shone forth from Mount Paran/With him were myriads of holy ones, / at his right, a host of his own." Putting aside the difficult words at the end of the verse, the opening of Moses's Blessings establishes a similar path for God's journey to the one in the Song of Deborah. Here too, Sinai is associated with Seir and Mt. Paran, that is to say, the southern part of eastern Jordan.

Another confirmation of God's arrival from that region is from the opening of the psalm at the end of The Book of Habakkuk (Habakkuk 3:3): "God came from Teman, /the Holy One from Mount Paran. Selah/ His glory covered the heavens, / and the earth was full of his praise."[9] Though Sinai, Edom, and Seir are not explicitly mentioned here, "Teman" and "Mt. Paran" appear as parallelism to Edom. In addition, "Teman" is a nickname for Edom. It means "south".[10]

---

[8] El-Masry et al. (2013).

[9] Though indeed it seems that most of the Book of Habakkuk was composed during the Babylonian era, the last chapter is an exception. It is not prophecy, but poetry. The general atmosphere of the prophecies of Habakkuk is one of distress stemming from the cruel Babylonian foe (see especially Habakkuk 1:6–17). A similar air of distress is also reflected in Habakkuk 3:2, 16–17. However, if we disregard those verses, we will find a victory poem in verses (Habakkuk 3:3–15, 18–19) that describes salvation and joy, and which is very different from the feel of the rest of the book. Because of this many have thought that the psalm in Habakkuk 3 is an ancient poem which was attributed to Habakkuk the Prophet by the book's editors. For a survey of the opinions regarding the composition and dating of the book, see Andersen (2001, 24–27); on the make-up and origin of the psalm in Habakkuk 3, see the survey there, 259–264.

[10] Amos 1:11–12, Obadiah 1:8–9, Jeremiah 49, Ezekiel 25:13.

Likewise, in Habakkuk, volcanic activity accompanies the arrival of God from the south (Habakkuk 3:3, 6):

> "God came from Teman,
>   the Holy One from Mount Paran. *Selah*
> His glory covered the heavens,
>   and the earth was full of his praise…
> He stopped and shook the earth;
>   he looked and made the nations tremble.
> The eternal mountains were shattered;
>   along his ancient pathways
>   the everlasting hills sank low."

When God appears, the mountains are shattered and the hills sink low, just as in the Song of Deborah.

Another interesting element in Habakkuk is the presence of Cushan and Midian in verse Habakkuk 3:7: "I saw the tents of Cushan under affliction;/ the tent curtains of the land of Midian trembled." Though the words "under affliction" are hard to interpret, the parallelism between "the tents of Cushan" and "the tent curtains of the land of Midian" is important: There is another parallel between "Cushan" and "Midian" in the Torah: the Cushite woman that Moses married (Numbers 12:1). Though Second Temple literature created the stories of Moses's escape to the land of Cush and his marriage to the daughter of the king of Cush,[11] the truth is more modest, and the "Cushite woman" was in actuality, a Midianite, as is mentioned in Exodus 2:21–22; 18:2–5.[12]

The psalm in Habakkuk describes earthquakes and volcanic activity in the land of Midian. This is not necessarily surprising. The Torah connects Moses, and the beginnings of the faith of Israel with the Midianites. But who were the Midianites? Archeological finds from Midianite territory show that though it wasn't a literate society, it was in possession of advanced and thriving technology. As I will expand upon below, it seems that the Midianites were the cause of the decline of the very developed copper production in the Araba and southern Jordan. They created unique and astonishingly decorated ceramics. According to the distribution of the ceramic findings, it seems that the Midianites were centered in what is now northwest Saudi Arabia. A first production center was discovered in

---

[11] Schneider (2019).
[12] Ibn Ezra's interpretation of Numbers 12:1 is explicit on the matter.

Al-Qurayya and recently a similar center was discovered in the ancient oasis in Tayma.[13] Midianite ceramics have also been found in copper mines and the big metal production centers in Timna and Finan in the eastern areas of the Araba (Finan is apparently the Biblical Punon). It seems then that Midianite culture was spread out between modern day northeast Saudi Arabia and outskirts of the Israel to the southeast. Essentially, the land of Midian, in its most broad sense, partially overlapped with Edom and Seir.[14] This is, as mentioned above, is an especially volcanic region. There is a clear congruence between these facts and the poetic descriptions of God's appearance in the Hebrew Bible.

And so, ancient poetry establishes the location of "Sinai" in a different location than the one that is reflected in the Torah literature. It is identified with the area between southeastern Jordan and modern-day northwestern Saudi Arabia. The appearance of God is accompanied by natural phenomena that fit the volcanic characteristics of this area. On the other hand, the location of Mt. Sinai- Horeb in the Torah—the area between the western Negev and Egypt, does not fit this description. There are no remnants of volcanic activity in the area referred to today as "the Sinai Desert". The affinity of Mt. Sinai in the poems with southern Jordan and the lands of Edom and Midian is interesting in light of what is known to us from other contexts regarding the importance of those lands in the traditions about the beginnings of Israel's faith.

BIBLIOGRAPHY

N. Amzallag, 2014, "Some Implications of the Vulcanic Theophany of YHWH on His Primeval Identity", *Antiguo Oriente* 12, 11–38.

F.I. Andersen, 2001, *Habakkuk* (AB), New York NY.

C. Echols, 2008, *"Tell Me O Muse": The Song of Deborah (Judges 5) in the Light of Heroic Poetry*, New York-London.

N.N. El-Masry et al., 2013, "Historical Accounts of the AD 1256 Eruption near Al-Madina", *Vorisa Scientific Meeting (November 17–18 2013) Conference Paper*, 9–13.

[13] See, Luciani (2016). On the Midianite ceramics in general, see, Knauf (1988, 15–25); Rothenberg and Glass (1983); and more recently, Luciani (2018).

[14] On the location of Midian see Knauf, ibid., 1–6. In addition, see the recent detailed survey by Miller (2021, 18–60, 115–146), regarding the land of Midian and the ritual sites discovered there.

R.D. Holmstedt, 2014, "Analyzing זֶה Grammar and Reading זֶהTexts of Ps 68:9 and Judg 5:5", *JHS* 14, 27pp.

E.A. Knauf, *Midian*, Wiesbaden, 1988.

I. Knohl, 2023, "THE SONG OF DEBORAH: HUMAN HEROISM OR DIVINE SALVATION", *Reshit: Studies in Judaism 7*, 1–22.

M. Leunenberger, 2010, "Jhwhs Herkunft aus dem Süden. Archäologische Befunde-biblische Überlieferungen — historische Korrelationen", *ZAW* 122, 1–19.

M. Leunenberger, 2017, "YHWH's Provenance from the South: A New Evaluation of the Arguments pro and contra", in: J. van Oorschot and M. Witte (eds.), The Origins of Yahwism (BZAW 484), Berlin-Boston, 157–179.

M. Luciani, 2016, "Mobility, Contacts and definition of Culture(s) in New Archeological Research in North East Arabia", in M. Luciani (ed.), *The Archeology of North Arabiah*, Vienna, 21–57.

M. Luciani, 2018, "Pottery from the "Midianite Heartland"? On Tell Kheleifeh and Qurayyah Painted Ware. New Evidence from the Harvard Semitic Museum", in: L. Nehmé & A. Al-Jallad, *To the Madbar and Back Again (Fs. M.C.A Macdonald)*, Leiden, 392–438.

R.D. Miller II, 2021, *Yahweh: Origin of a Desert God* (FRLANT 284), Göttingen.

H. Pfeiffer, 2005, *Jahwes Kommen von Süden: Jdc 5; Hab 3; Dtn 33 und Ps 68 in ihrem literatur- und theologiegeschichtlicen Umfeld* (FRLANT 211), Göttingen.

B. Rothenberg & J. Glass, 1983, 'The Midianite Pottery', in J.F.A. Sawyer & D.J.A. Clines (eds.) *Midian, Moab and Edom: The History and Archaeology of Late Bronze and Iron Age Jordan and North-West Arabia* (JSOTSup. 24), Sheffield, 65–124.

S. Schneider, 2019, "Moses in Cush", *Jewis Bible Quarterly*, 47, 113–119.

CHAPTER 4

Mt. Sinai and the Midianites-Kenites

The Song of Deborah describes God's journey from Seir: (Judges 5:4): "LORD, when you went out from Seir, / when you marched from the region of Edom." What is the connection between these areas and God? Is this indeed the place where God permanently resides and from where He departs? An Egyptian document from the fourteenth century B.C.E. could help answer these questions. It was during this time that the famous Pharoah Akhenaten revolutionized Egyptian religion. However, we are not interested in Akhenaten, but rather his father, Amenhotep III. Amenhotep III ruled in the first half of the fourteenth century B.C.E and was a mighty ruler. A few geographic lists from his time have survived. They deal with war campaigns to various locations, including Jordan, among other places. One of these lists describes settlements or groups who dwelled around Edom and Seir.[1] The list describes the districts that were home to nomads called the "Shasu" in Egyptian. The term may be connected to the Hebrew word *šôsîm* robbers, or may stem from Egyptian itself.[2] Whatever the case, the Shasu were nomadic tribes who lived in tents. In modern day terms we would perhaps describe them as Bedouins. So, the list mentions nomadic tribes who live in the region of southern Jordan. In addition, this list and a similar list from the days of Ramses II (the thirteenth century B.C.E.) mention the term "the Land of the Shasu,

---

[1] See, most recently, the comprehensive discussion by Fleming (2020, 23–62).
[2] See the discussion in Miller (2021, 79–81).

© The Author(s), under exclusive license to Springer Nature Switzerland AG 2024
I. Knohl, *Biblical Sinai traditions*,
https://doi.org/10.1007/978-3-031-77983-1_4

Seir". Meaning nomadic tribes who live in the region of Seir. Then the
text denotes the lands of the Shasu *y, h, w*. Meaning, the lands of the
nomads whose tribe name, or the name of the region they live in is sym-
bolized by the Egyptian letters parallel to *y, h, w*. The Egyptian language
has only consonants and no vowels. We do not know exactly how to pro-
nounce the name but we do know that the *w* does not indicate a vowel.
That is to say, not, YAHO, but YEHAVE, YEHOVA, YEHOVE or something like that. It is clear that this is a name that is similar to God's name
yhwh- the pronunciation of which is also unclear. If we glean the information found in the early poetry and combine it with the information from
the Egyptian documents, we can see that there is a connection between
these two sources. In the Song of Deborah *yhwh* is described as arriving
from Seir, and in the Egyptian lists, the land of the *yhw* nomads is mentioned in proximity to Seir.[3]

The Kenite theory, a theory in Hebrew Biblical scholarship that
espouses that the source of the faith in *yhw* is connected to the Midianites
or their relatives the Kenites, precedes the discovery of the Egyptian list.[4]
However, the discovery of the list as well as a similar list from the days of
Ramses II, lends significant support to the opinion that the god, "*yhw*"
was worshipped by these tribes even before the time of Moses. (It is estimated that Moses lived during the thirteenth century B.C.E. The list from
the time of Amenhotep predates him by a century). So, when the poems
describe *yhwh* departing from His place in Seir or Edom, it is possible that
this is indeed the original location where God was known and worshipped.

---

[3] Recently Rachel Shlomi Chen (Shlomi Chen 2021) cast doubt on the contributions of
these notations to the history of religion in the Hebrew Bible. However, I reject her doubts
because the comparison she made to the mentions of the Canaanite gods in Egyptian culture
is methodologically flawed. What she discusses is not even close to proof. The Canaanite
religion was known in Egypt from the days of the Hyksos, as we can see, for instance, from
the identification of the Canaanite gods with Egyptian gods (see, for instance, Goldwasser
2006). This familiarity is also reflected in the stele that Ramses II erected to mark 400 years
of the rule of Baal-Seth in Egypt. In light of this, it is clear that the characterization of the
Canaanite gods with divine elements in these lists, and similarly, the appearance of divine
elements next to place names with Canaanite theophoric elements of gods that are known in
Egypt (such as Beith Anath or Beith Dagon) can be understood. Things are different when
it comes to the Shasu, who were less well-known in Egypt, and so both their religion and the
names of their gods were puzzles to the Egyptian scribes. It is no wonder then that in these
cases there is no denotation of divinity.

[4] For this history of this theory, see, most recently, Fleming (2020, 67–100), as well as
Blenkinsopp's lucid survey, 2008.

If we accept this line of thinking, a number of things open for us. It could explain why the Tetragram was revealed to Moses specifically when he was shepherding sheep for his father-in-law, Jethro the Priest of Midian. As mentioned above, Midian, Seir and Edom partially overlap. The Midianites settled in Seir and Edom, and also south of there, in modern day northwest Saudi Arabia. If the Midianites did indeed live there, as can be inferred from the poem in Habakkuk 3 and the line- "the tent curtains of the lands of Midian" in the context of God's arrival from Teman, the story in Exodus 3 can be seen in a new light. Moses was shepherding in the Midianite region when the Tetragram YHWH was revealed to him next to the burning bush.[5]

There have been many varied suggestions made for understanding the revelation of the Tetragram, as well as its relationship to the religions of other regional cultures, such as Canaan or Babylonia. However, they are useless suggestions. YHWH is not a part of the pantheon of Canaan or Babylonia, nor does He appear in contemporary Canaanite or Babylonian religious texts. He is also alien to the Egyptian pantheon. Indeed, it is possible that when Moses came to Pharoah speaking in the name of God, and the Egyptian king replied, (Exodus 5:2) "I do not know the Lord", these were not empty words.

So, the name *yhwh* is not connected Egyptian or Babylonian culture. Even Canaanite culture, which is similar to Biblical Hebrew culture, and has a lot of affinity to it, to the extent of joint names for God, such as *el*, even it is not familiar with the name *yhwh*. If this is the case, then the name *yhwh* is not of the large cultures of the ancient near east. Rather it is only known in a small southeastern corner of the region. There, according to the Egyptian lists mentioned above, they knew *yhwh* even before Moses did.

This is somewhat of a surprise. What we may conceive of as the unequivocal foundation and most unique aspect of the religion of the Hebrew Bible, the divine name, the holiest name, *yhwh*, was not revealed first to the Children of Israel, but had been previously revealed to the Midianites. In my opinion there is a hint to this in the Hebrew Bible itself. The Rabbis say that Jethro the Priest of Midian had seven names.[6] How did they reach this conclusion? In various places in the Hebrew Bible Jethro is referred to

---

[5] Regarding Hebrew Biblical traditions about the source of the gods of Israel in Midian see, Weisman (1978); Weinfeld (1987). Recently Roi has sought to track the main local characteristics of the Sinai traditions Roi (2020).

[6] Mekhilta DeRabbi Ishmael, Jethro, The Horovitz-Rabin edition, pg. 189.

by a number of different names. That is the basis for the Rabbinic statement. One of those names is KAYIN. Here I will point to two relevant
texts. Judges 1:16:

> The descendants of Hobab the Kenite, Moses's father-in-law, went up with
> the people of Judah from the city of palms into the wilderness of Judah,
> which lies in the Negeb near Arad.

In this text Moses's father-in-law is referred to as "the Kenite", and we are
told that his descendants went up from the city of palms. The identity of
the city of palms is uncertain; there are those who have suggested Jericho,
while others, Ein Gedi. In any case, the Kenites went up from the city of
palms to the Judean wilderness, in the Negeb near Arad and settled there.
And indeed, there is an archeological site near Arad called "Horvat Uza".
However, some scholars have indicated that the name of the site is incor-
rect, and that the site should be identified with the town of Kinah (Joshua
15:22). The nearby wadi is called Wadi al Kinah, and this is essentially the
area in which the Kenites settled.[7]

Further on in the Book of Judges, we read (Judges 4:11):

> Now Heber the Kenite had separated from KAYIN, that is, the descendants
> of Hobab the father-in-law of Moses, and had encamped as far away as Elon-
> bezaanannim, which is near Kedesh.

Heber the Kenite, the husband of Yael, separated from the "KAYIN".
Who is "Kayin"? He is to be associated with the descendants of Hobab
Moses's father-in-law. In the previous quotation Moses's father-in-law was
called "The Kenite", but here he is called "Hobab", a name familiar to us
from a similar context in Numbers 10:29. Whatever the case, the writer of
Judges 4:11 connects Moses's father-in-law and "KAYIN". Meaning,
there is a group called the Kenites, or KAYIN", who are associated with
Moses's father-in-law. We can say with some assurance that the Kenites
were a sub-group of Midianites, because Jethro was a priest of Midian.

When we consider the first chapters of the Book of Genesis an interesting picture regarding the Divine names arises. Only the name *Elohim* is
used throughout the first creation story in Chap. 1 up until the passage

---

[7] Regarding Horvat Uza and its connection to the Kenites and their settlements see Ahituv
(1995, 254), as well as Na'aman (2016).

about Shabbat at the beginning of Chap. 2. From 2:4 on both Divine names are used together:

> These are the generations of the heavens and the earth when they were created. In the day that the Lord *yhwh* God *Elohim* made the earth and the heavens.

So too is the case in most of the second creation story; the story of Eden, and Adam and Eve's sin. As is well known, critical scholarship of the Torah explains the transition from the use of the name *Elohim* in Genesis 1 to *yhwh* later as proof of a change in sources. Whatever the case, Genesis 4:1 tells of the following occurrence:

> Now the man knew his wife Eve, and she conceived and bore Cain, saying, "I have produced a man with the help of the Lord. [*qānîtî ʾîš ʾet yhwh*]

This is the first birth in human history: Eve gives birth to a son and calls him Cain—"KAYIN". She explains his name in the following way: "I have produced a man with the help of the Lord." The verb *qānîtî* is used here in its meaning as "I produced" such as in, "God Most High, maker of heaven and earth" (Genesis 14:19) [*qoneh šāmayim wāʾāreṣ*]. This is the first time that the Tetragram is uttered by a human. The name Cain— "KAYIN" appears and then is explicitly connected with the Divine name, *yhwh*.

If we consider this in light of Judges, KAYIN, Moses's father-in-law, and the Kenites, we can see that according to the teller of the story of Cain's birth long before Abraham, Moses, and Israel, at the dawn of human history the Kenites knew the name *yhwh* and were associated with that name.

Cain is a tragic figure. He was the first person to sacrifice to God and establish ritual worship; he was the first person to take of the fruits of the land and serve it up as a sacrifice. And yet, it was his younger brother, Abel's sacrifice that was accepted by God, while his was rejected. In his jealousy and anger, he murdered his brother. As a punishment Cain was cursed to wander. He had previously worked the earth, but from then on was fated to wander, to and fro. This is the mythological reasoning for why the Kenites and Midianites were nomadic tribes: because their forefather, Cain, was cursed- "you will be a fugitive and a wanderer on the earth" (Genesis 4:12).

Later, the Book of Genesis tells of the descendants of Cain and his descendants' descendants, including of the interesting figure of Lamech, the first of the Biblical poets. One of Lamech's descendants is mentioned in Genesis 4:22: "Zillah bore Tubal-cain, who made all kinds of cooper and iron tools." That is to say that there was a child named Tubal-cain. The meaning of his name is somewhat opaque,[8] however, whatever the case, Cain is a central part of his name. Tubal-cain was a refiner or tool-maker meaning, someone who produces bronze and iron. This means that even at this early period of time in human history, the descendants of Cain, or at least one of them who also bears the name Cain (Tubal-cain), were connected to working with cooper. As I mentioned, the Midianites, and the Kenites were experts in cooper production; in Edom, the Araba, and Timna. And so, some of the most explicit characteristics of Kenite/Midianite society are already noted in Genesis, at the dawn of humanity. They are nomads who work in, among other things, the production of cooper, and they are connected to the name *yhwh*. All of these little details reinforce the hypothesis that this is the group from whom early Israel became familiar with the Tetragram, *yhwh*.[9]

Nissim Amzaleg has connected the volcanic character of God's revelation with the profession of the Midianites-Kenites, the first *yhwh* worshippers, as producers of cooper.[10] According to his theory, the volcanic eruption during God's appearance represents a kiln. As it says in Exodus 19:18: "Now all of Mount Sinai was wrapped in smoke, because the LORD had descended upon it in fire; the smoke went up like the smoke of a kiln."

* * *

We can now summarize what we know about the origin of the Sinai tradition, its connection to the Midianite-Kenite cultures, and the possible

---

[8] In Ezekiel (27:13) the city of Tubal in Anatolia is mentioned in connection with trade in bronze. See, Ahituv, Tubal-Qain.

[9] Another sign of the connection between the Kenites and metal production can be found in Arabic, in which the noun, Cain, (القَيْن), means "a blacksmith, ironworker". (See the entry on this word in Lisan al-Arab). For more on the Kenites and Midianites, their wanderings, and the area they lived in, their connection to the production of metal and metalworking, on the one hand, and the source of Israel's God, on the other, see, Abramsky (1954); Amzalleg (2009); Kleiman et al. (2017). See also, Kalimi's hesitant evaluation of this issue,.1980

[10] See his article mentioned in the previous footnote, as well as Amzallag (2014, 2015).

implications of these, the revelation of the Tetragram, and the worship of God in those cultures.

Sinai in old Hebrew Biblical poems is not a term for the Sinai Peninsula which does not have the necessary volcanic characteristics. Instead, we should be looking for Sinai of the poems in the volcanic regions in the northwestern Arabian Peninsula, or in southern Jordan. Apparently, *yhwh* was known and worshipped in this area, and we can make assumptions regarding His characteristics and identity via what we know about the local cultures. The central foundation that marks the appearance of *yhwh* in these traditions is volcanic activity that is expressed with fire and earthquakes. This can be seen even beyond Hebrew Biblical poetry, in the story of the revelation at Sinai in Exodus 19. It is possible, as Amzaleg suggests, that the fire and smoke that are characteristic of descriptions of these phenomena, described in the Hebrew bible as a "kiln" (Exodus 19:18), and a "smoking oven" (Genesis 15:17. Compare to Isaiah 31:9) hint at the Midianite's profession as smelters and producers of copper, and maybe even testify to an essential-primary relationship between the god *yhwh* and copper production.[11] Another possible direction is that the sight of the fire, smoke, and furnaces were symbols for God's exploding jealousy, jealousy that, according to Goitein's theory, is the meaning of the Divine name.[12]

---

[11] Amzalleg, ibid. Reservations regarding the Kenite theory have recently been expressed by Frevel (2021). According to him, the appearance of Yawhistic theophoric names among the kings descended from Omri, proves that the kings of the House of Ahab were the ones who turned God into the national God, and it is under their influence that His worship spread to Judah as well. However, he has an arbitrary relationship with the sources. As he knows (pg. 9 in his article), theophoric names like these had been found in Israel and Judah according to the documentation of the Hebrew Bible, and before the rise of Omri (so too, Abijah son of Rehoboam in Judah, and Baasha the son of Ahjiah in Israel). However, Frevel declines to relate to this finding. Even more so, Yawhistic names that were recorded in the House of Saul (Jonathan-Jahonathan, Ishvah-Ishvi), and David's court (Joab son of Zeruiah, Benayahu son of Jehoiadia, Jonadab son of Shimeah, Adonijah son of Haggith). Their appearance alongside Ba'alist names (such as Mephibosheth-Mephiba'al, Ishbosheth-Ishba'al) is proof of the credibility of the tradition regarding personal names that were common among the courts of the early kings. This tradition preserved the remanence of the name *yhwh* as early as those generations alongside the syncretism that was then common in Israel (for more, see, de Moor 1990, 10–41; Rofé 2015). Frevel, however, does not refer to these at all, and does not explain his negations.

[12] Goitein (1956).

BIBLIOGRAPHY

S. Abramsky, 1954, "The Qenites", *EI* 3 (1954), 116–124 [in Hebrew].

S. Ahituv, 1995, *Joshua* (Mikra Leyisrael), Tel Aviv 1995 [in Hebrew].

N. Amzalleg, 2009, "Yahweh, the Canaanite God of Metallurgy?", *JSOT* 33, 387–404.

N. Amzallag, 2014, "Some Implications of the Vulcanic Theophany of YHWH on His Primeval Identity", *Antiguo Oriente* 12, 11–38.

N. Amzallag, 2015, "The Origin and Evolution of the Saraph Symbol", *Antiguo Oriente* 13, 99–126.

J. Blenkinsopp, 2008, "The Midianite-Kenite Hypothesis Revisited and the Origins of Judah", *JSOT* 33, 131–153.

D. Fleming, 2020, *Yahweh before Israel*, Cambridge.

C. Frevel, 2021, "When and from Where did YHWH Emerge? Some Reflections on Early Yahwism in Israel and Judah", *Entangled Religions* 12.2: *The Desert Origins of God: Yahweh's Emergence and Early History in the Southern Levant and Northern Arabia* (32pp.).

D. Goitein, 1956, "YHWH the Passionate: The Monotheistic Meaning and Origin of the Name YHWH", *VT* 6, 1–9.

O. Goldwasser, 2006, "King Apophis of Avaris and the Emergence of Monotheism", in: E. Czerny et al. (eds.), *Timelines: Studies in Honour of Manfred Bietak* (Orientalia Lovaniensia Analecta 149), I-III, Leuven, II, 129–133.

S. Kleiman, A. Kleiman and E. Ben-Yosef, 2017, "Metalworers' Material Culture in the Early Iron Age Levant: The Ceramic Assemblage from Site 34 (Slave's Hill) in the Timna Valley", *Tel Aviv* 44, 232–264.

R.D. Miller II, 2021, *Yahweh: Origin of a Desert God* (FRLANT 284), Göttingen.

J.C. de Moor, 1990, *The Rise of Yahwism: The Roots of Israelite Monotheism*, Leuven.

N. Na'aman, 2016, "The 'Kenite Hypothesis' in the Light of the Excavations at Horvat 'Uza", in: G. Bartoloni & M.G. Biga (eds.), *Not Only History*, Winona Lake IN, 171–182.

A. Rofé, 2015, "Text and Context: The Textual Elimination of the Names of Gods and its Literary, Administrative, and Legal Context", in: C. Warman (ed.), *From Author to Copyist; Essays on the Composition, Redaction, and Transmission of the Hebrew Bible in Honor of Zipi Talshir*, Winona Lake, IN, 63–79.

M. Roi, 2020, ""You Shall Worship God on This Mountain" (Exod 3:12) as a Key to Revealing the Roots of the Sinai Covenant", *Beit Mikra* 65, 138–163 [in Hebrew].

R. Shlomi Hen, 2021, "Signs of YHWH, God of the Hebrews, in New Kingdom Egypt?", *Entangled Religions* 12, 16pp.

M. Weinfeld, 1987, "The Traditions about Moses and Jethro at the Mount of God", *Tarbiz* 56, 449–460.

Z. Weisman, 1978, "The Mountain of God", *Tarbiz* 47, 107–119 [in Hebrew].

CHAPTER 5

Tablets and Covenant in Ancient Poetry

So, there is an established location for Mt. Sinai in the descriptions of Divine revelation in ancient poetry, whether as the place of God's origin (Deut. 33:2), or whether as one of the mountains that quaked as He appeared (Judges 5:5; compare to Psalms 68:9). The question then arises: did the poetic tradition in the Hebrew Bible also preserve a memory of the Divine revelation inherent in the giving of laws and a covenant between God and His nation? This question becomes more acute in light of the central place of the revelation at Sinai- Horeb in the narrative tradition of the Torah.[1] The early date of the oral poetry as well as the expansion of literacy in Israel and Judah as late as the eighth century BCE, and the relative lateness of the written narratives in the Hebrew Bible, make it necessary to clarify what stand the poetic tradition takes regarding the giving of the laws at Sinai. In other words, does it articulate the occasion of the

---

[1] This is also the case in the earliest tradition, the pre-priestly one, which is also identified with Documents E and J (Exodus 11–24, 32–34), as well as the Deuteronomistic tradition, and which refers to Sinai as "Horeb" (Deuteronomy 5:2). The totality of these traditions assume that the first covenant was broken during the Sin of the Golden Calf (Exodus 32, Deut. 8–21) and was renewed afterwards (Exodus 33–32, Deut. 8:21–10:11). The priestly tradition in all its variations also describes the giving of the law and the covenant at Sinai (Exodus 19:1–2).

© The Author(s), under exclusive license to Springer Nature 29
Switzerland AG 2024
I. Knohl, *Biblical Sinai traditions,*
https://doi.org/10.1007/978-3-031-77983-1_5

giving of the law and the covenant at Sinai, and thus it indicates an early date for this tradition?[2]

As mentioned above, the poetic tradition establishes Sinai's location in the region of Edom and Seir, which is relatively far from Egypt. On the other hand, the Torah narrative, across all its sources, assumes that the site of Mt. Sinai is close to Egypt, and is only a few months' journey away (see, for instance, the priestly tradition in Exodus 19:1–2). The Israelite camp would only reach Edom and Mt. Seir at the end of forty years of wandering in the desert (Numbers 20:12–23, Deut. 2:4–8).[3] That is to say that the various narratives identify the location of Sinai-Horeb somewhere else, far from its location in the poetic tradition.

It is evident that the Torah traditions and the poetic traditions diverge regarding the geographical location of Mt. Sinai-Horeb. Similarly, there are divergences in the content of the traditions, especially concerning the giving of the law and the covenant between God and His people, as can be seen below.

THE SONG OF DEBORAH (JUDGES 5) AND PSALMS 68

In the Song of Deborah the poet turns to the Kings of Canaan (Judges 5:3–4): "Hear, O kings; give ear, O princes;/ to the Lord I will sing;/ I will make melody to the Lord, the God of Israel./ Lord, when you went out from Seir,/ when you marched from the region of Edom, / the earth trembled,/ and the heavens poured;/ the clouds indeed poured water." The poet stresses to the Kings of Canaan that the Lord that they seek to praise is not of Canaan and its culture. He is foreign to them. His origin is in Seir and Edom, that nomadic arena that is extraterritorial to Canaanite culture.

There is no refined or perfect monotheism in the Song of Deborah. There is no claim that *yhwh* is the only God. However, He is the only god that is mentioned in the poem as the God of Israel and Israel is called, "people of *yhwh*" (Judges 5:11). As mentioned above, the Song of Deborah is one of the oldest compositions in the Hebrew Bible, and it is

---

[2] My general position on the early date of the poetry discussed here was presented above in Chap. 3, footnote 1. See the literature there.

[3] There is no reason to discuss the issue of the Israelites journey from Egypt to Canaan according to the various Torah sources (see Haran 1973, 37–76). However, according to all the sources the revelation at Mt. Sinai/Horeb occurred at the beginning of their journey. Their arrival in the land of Edom occurred towards the end.

possible that it was written close to the time of the events it describes, around 1100 B.C.E.

Though indeed the Song of Deborah describes God's ascent from Seir and the Field of Edom, and Mt. Sinai quaking before Him, there is no mention of a covenant or the giving of laws to Israel at Sinai. A parallel to this can be found in Psalms 68. This psalm is mostly early, though it does contain some later additions.[4] The description in the psalm is very close, structurally speaking and in terms of content to the one in the Song of Deborah (Psalms 68:7–8): "O God, when you went out before your people,/ when you marched through the wilderness, *Selah*/ the earth quaked, the heavens poured down rain/ at the presence of God, the God of Sinai,/ at the presence of God, the God of Israel." Here too, God appears, marching from Sinai, without mention of the giving of laws or the making of a covenant at Sinai.

HABAKUK 3

Another poem that should be examined is Habakuk 3 (3–7):

> God came from Teman,
>   the Holy One from Mount Paran. *Selah*
> His glory covered the heavens,
>   and the earth was full of his praise.
> The brightness was like the sun;
>   rays came forth from his hand,
>   where his power lay hidden.
> Before him went pestilence,
>   and plague followed close behind.
> He stopped and shook the earth;
>   he looked and made the nations tremble.
> The eternal mountains were shattered;
>   along his ancient pathways
>   the everlasting hills sank low.
> I saw the tents of Cushan under affliction;
>   the tent curtains of the land of Midian trembled.

The piece is full of difficult phrases, but its context is clear: it describes nature trembling and excitement in the land of Midian as God appears,

---

[4] See, Knohl (2012b).

similarly to what is described in the Song of Deborah and Psalms 68. Here too, there is no mention of laws or a covenant at Sinai. The text gives a spectacular description of the volcanic activity erupting as God reveals Himself.

MOSES'S BLESSINGS (DEUT. 33)

An additional piece of poetry relevant to our interests is Moses's Blessings in Deut. 33. Unlike the poems discussed above, the opening of the Blessing (Deut. 33:1–5) contains phrases and concepts that seem to hint to law and the giving of the Torah at Sinai. We will discuss them in order.

First, we must clarify the Qeri and Ketiv of the word ʾašdot in Deut. 33:2. The Qeri splits the word in two, and reads, ʾeš dāt, meaning, the God who came from Sinai gave the flame of law to Israel. On the face of it, the text is referring to the giving of the Torah at Sinai.

However, there is reason to doubt the precedence of the Qeri. First of all, the word ʾešdāt is planted in the middle of the theophanic description that continues into verse 3. The historical survey in Moses's Blessings only begins in verses 4–5. Meaning the supposed reference to the giving of the law is in the wrong place. Secondly, the Ketiv word, ʾašdot, can actually be well understood as a part of the theophanic notations and geographic descriptions in verses 2–3. There are those who suggest that the word indicates a river, similar to ʾ ṣ̌ed hanehâlyim (the slopes of the wadis) in Numbers 21:15, and ʾašdôt hapisgâ (the lower slopes of Pisgah) (Deut. 3:17)[5] However, the opinion that this is a description of the Divine radiance, perhaps as part of the volcanic phenomena that characterize His revelation in the poetic description is more likely. This opinion is supported by the word "ʾšḏ" in Syriac which denotes streams of light and fire.[6]

Another reason to dismiss the Qeri reading, ʾeš dāt, in Deut. 33:2, comes from the historical framework of Moses's Blessing. The blessings reinforce the positions of the tribes of Joseph, Ephraim, and Menashe, (Deut. 33:13–17), while the tribe of Judah is given a minor role (32:7). It seems correct to assume that the origin of the poem is in the northern tribes of Israel. This means it could not have been composed, either partially or completely, after the destruction of Northern Kingdom and its

---

[5] See for instance, Rofé (1978, 237–239).
[6] Seeligmann (1964, 191, 195). Compare this in this context, to Habakkuk 3:4: "rays came forth from His hands".

capital Samaria in 720 BCE.[7] Though the separation of *ʾeš dāṯ*, is nicely symbolic,[8] the source of the word *dat*, is Persian, and is only found in later Hebrew Biblical literature (see, for instance, Esther 9:14). The Persian influence on the language of the Hebrew Bible began no earlier than the sixth century B.C.E and cannot be reconciled with the much earlier northern source that is reflected in the lion's share of the poem.

Thus, it seems that the separation of *ʾešdāṯ* into two words is the work of an editor- a late copyist, who was active no earlier than the Persian period. The editor felt that the Torah revelation at Mt. Sinai was not adequately represented in the Blessings and found a hint to it in the mysterious word *ʾešdāṯ*.

Apparently, this edit was part of a broader trend towards alterations of Moses's Blessings. This trend also probably includes the clear reference to the giving of the Torah in Deut. 33:4 ("Moses charged us with the law/ as a possession for the assembly of Jacob"). However, this text is somewhat suspicious especially when considering its context: First, grammatically, the word "us", is in first person plural, which is in contrast to the references to the nation and tribes in third person throughout the whole poem. Secondly, the phrase "the assembly of Jacob" is also suspect linguistically. Though the word קהל" assembly" is common in Biblical Hebrew, the female form "*qehilâh*" only appears once more, in Nehemia 5:6. The diversion from the regular use of third person in the poem, as well as its proximity of "*qehilâh*" to late Biblical Hebrew means that there is reason to assume that Deut. 33:4 is a later addition to Moses's Blessings from the Persian period. Just like *ʾeš dāṯ* in verse 2, this addition also seeks to emphasize the place of the Torah in the ancient poem. These two late interventions are proof that the lack of the Torah and a covenant in the reference to God's arrival from Sinai isn't an artificial problem. Even earlier scribes were suspicious of it.

It is possible that there is another hint to the giving of the laws and commandments in the continuation of the description of Divine revelation at the opening of Moses's Blessings: ישא מדברתיך. This difficult phrase may hint at the Divine law.[9] However, its context proves that it must be

---

[7] For a longer discussion regarding the date of this poem, see Appendix A.

[8] The comparison of the Torah to fire and a description of it being written in white and black fire appear in the Jerusalem Talmud Sheqalim 6A, 49d.

[9] This is the opinion of the Rabbis and the medieval commentators such as Rashi and Rabbi Ibn Ezra.

referring to something else. The phrase is located in the middle of an obscure verse[10] that can be divided into four hemistiches:

Indeed the beloved one of peoples   all his holy ones are at your hand
and they bow themselves at your feet   he carries your pronouncements.

The verse describes God's war against the nations or gods, as can be found in other descriptions of God's arrival from Sinai (compare to Habakkuk 3:4 etc. Psalms 68:22 on).[11] The second half of the verse focuses on the vanquishing of God's foes. The difficult phrase "he carries your pronouncement" can then be explained via parallelism.

The hemistich "they bow themselves at your feet" is a description of God's foes being crushed beneath His feet.[12] So, the parallel hemistich, "he carries your pronouncement", must continue the description of defeat. This tableau can also be seen in parallel texts from the ancient Near East. A similar description appears in Letter 256 of the El-Amarna letters. Abi-milku the King of Tyre expresses his loyalty to Pharoah in the following way (line 39): "On my stomach and on my back, I bear the words of the King, my master".[13]

Another proof of the fact that the phrase, "he carries your pronouncement", describes the defeat of God's enemies stems from the parallel between the opening of Moses's Blessings and its closing (Deut. 33:29):

Happy are you, O Israel! Who is like you,
    a people saved by the LORD,
    the shield of your help

[10] Many commentators have noted the difficult nature of the text. It is therefore no wonder that Steuernagel (1923, 123) decided that that the text is meaningless in its current form ("Der gegenwärtige Text ergiebt keinen Sinn").

[11] On descriptions of wars between the gods in Deut. 33, see Seeligmann (1964, 200), as well as Knohl (2012a).

[12] It is difficult to determine between all the various etymologies and subtleties of the meanings of the verb *tukú*. See HALOT *tkh*. There are those who have suggested interpreting it in light of Arabic, as "fell, lay down". Komlós suggests that the etymology of the verb comes from its Aramaic parallel, *tkk*, which means "to bind." In this case the verse would mark the binding of God's enemies as was customary among the kings of the ancient Near East who are described binding their defeated foes. See, Komlós (1956).

[13] See, Tigay (2016, vol. II, 818).

and the sword of your triumph!
Your enemies shall come fawning to you,
    but you shall tread on their backs.

The verse ends with the following picture: Israel has overcome their eneies, and they are laid down on the ground (alive or dead) while Israel treads on their backs.[14]

It seems then, that the parallel phrases "and they bow themseleves at your feet/ he carries your pronouncements" at the beginning of the poem do not refer to the giving of the law to Israel because they appear in the context of a description of God's war against His foes and their defeat. The context does not involve law.

* * *

This investigation into the early poetic descriptions of God's arrival from Sinai proves that they lack the narrative's emphasis on the Torah. They do not contain, in their original versions, any mention of giving laws or Torah or to a covenant between God and His nation at Sinai, even though these are the heart of the narrative tradition in the Torah. According to early poetry, God goes out and marches from Sinai, but does not reveal Himself verbally there.

BIBLIOGRAPHY

David N. Freedman, 1980, "The Poetic Structure of the Framework of Deuteronomy 33", in: G.A. Rendsburg et al. (eds.), *The Bible World (Fs. Cyrus H. Gordon)*, New York, 25–46.

M. Haran, 1973, הרן, מ' ., *Ages and institutions in the Bible*, Tel Aviv. תקופות ומוסדות בתקופת המקרא: עיונים היסטוריים, תל אביב

I. Knohl, 2012a, "God's Victory over 'the Olden Gods': Theological Corrections in Deuteronomy 33.12,27", in: F.H. Polak and A. Brenner (eds.), *Words, Ideas, Worlds; Biblical Essays in Honour of Yairah Amit*, Sheffield, 145–149.

I. Knohl, 2012b, "Psalm 68: Structure, Composition and Geography", *JHS* 12, 22pp.

O. Komlós, 1956, " תכו לרגלך (Deut. XXXIII 3)", *VT* 6, 435–436.

---

[14] Regarding the parallel between the opening of Moses's Blessings to its closing, and the continuity between them see Freedman (1980, 30–35).

א' רופא, "ברכת משה, מקדש נבו ושאלת מוצא הלוויים (דב' ל"ג)", בתוך: ספר, 1978,Rofé
ש"א ליונשטם, ירושלים 424; נדפס–תשל"ח, 409 שנית אצל הנ"ל, מבוא לספר דברים, ירושל
ים –249תשמ"ח, 234.

I.L. Seeligmann, 1964, "A Psalm from Pre-Regal Times", *VT* 14, 75–92.

C. Steuernagel, 1923, *Die Bücher Deuteronomium und Josua* 2 (GHAT), Göttingen.

J.H. Tigay, 2016, Deuteronomy (Mikra Leyisrael), vol. I–II, Tel Aviv.

CHAPTER 6

Revelation and the Covenant and Its Breaking at the Waters of Meribah

A

Our investigation into early poetry indicates that the tradition regarding the arrival of God from Sinai and Seir is a separate tradition from the one concerning the giving of law and the covenant at Sinai. So, we must now clarify to where God, coming up from the south, was going. Additionally, we must also clarify at what stage and location the poetic traditions establish His covenant with Israel.

The answer to these questions possibly lies in a description preserved in Levi's blessing in Deut. 33:8–11:[1]

> And of Levi he said,
>
> Give to Levi your Thummim
> and your Urim to your loyal one,
> whom you tested at Massah,

---

[1] There are scholars who believe that Levi's blessing is either completely or partially a secondary addition to the poem. However, in my opinion, the sophisticated narrative structure of the poem (see appendix A) proves that the whole poem (except for sporadic edits, most of which were discussed with above) is one harmonic creation that was composed among the Northern Tribes. As mentioned above, I accept the opinion that the blessings (33:6–25) and pieces of the framing of the piece (33:1–5, 26–29) are one composition. In this case as well, the harmonious narrative structure of the poem proves its general unity. See, Freedman (1980), and Appendix A.

I. Knohl, *Biblical Sinai traditions*,
https://doi.org/10.1007/978-3-031-77983-1_6

with whom you contended at the waters of Meribah,
who said of his father and mother,
  'I regard them not';
he ignored his kin
  and did not acknowledge his children.
For they observed your word
  and kept your covenant.
They teach Jacob your ordinances
  and Israel your law;
they place incense before you
  and whole burnt offerings on your altar.
Bless, O LORD, his substance,
  and accept the work of his hands;
crush the loins of his adversaries,
  of those who hate him, so that they do not rise again.

The blessing relates the reason that the Urim and Thumim were given to the Tribe of Levi, as well as the reason that the Levites were placed in charge of ritual and of teaching Torah to Israel.

The Urim and Thumim served as tools for divination in various circumstances. They are mentioned in both early and late sources in Hebrew Biblical literature. They served, among other things, in determining the judgement of Jonathan the son of Saul (I Samuel 14:41).[2] The Ephod, which held the Urim and Thumim was also used to plan military campaigns (see for instance, I Samuel 32; II Samuel 5:19–23; and cf. Ezekiel 21:26). The military use of the Urim and Thumim also appears quite clearly in the priestly tradition in Numbers 27:21 in which Israel's journeys were conducted according to the decisions of the Urim and Thumim borne by Elazar the son of Aaron the Priest.

Divination using the Urim and Thumim disappears after David's rule, and was replaced with other methods of inquiry, primarily prophecy (for instance I King 22; II Kings 3). This indicates that the reference to the Urim and Thumim in Levi's blessing is ancient and is proof of the early date of the description and the tradition described in it.[3] Proof of the relatively early date of the poem is also found in its northern roots. This can be seen in the marginal place of the Tribe of Judah, who are only allotted

---

[2] The text has been disrupted and should be amended. See Toeg's discussion, 1969.
[3] For more on the Urim and Thumim see Van Dam (1997, 7), and ibid., (169–176) regarding the Urim and Thumim being given to Levi in Moses's blessing as well as their role in teaching the ways of justice.

one verse in the piece relative to the centrality of the children of Josef who are allotted five verses.

The justification for giving the Urim and Thumim to the sons of Levi in Moses's Blessings is in the fact that they overcame a Divine test at Massah and the waters of Meribah (Deut. 33:8):

> Give to Levi your Thummim
> and your Urim to your loyal one,
> whom you tested at Massah,
> with whom you contended at the waters of Meribah.

The author is hinting to earlier events, known to the poet and their readers, in which God was aided by the sons of Levi during a conflict.[4] The primary narrative tradition about Massah and Meribah in the Torah (Exodus 17:1–7, Numbers 20;1–13) presents a reversed turn of events in which it is Israel that tests God. Echoes of this tradition can also be seen in Psalms 95:9 ("When your ancestors tested me/ and put me to the proof, though they had seen my work").

However, in addition to these narrative description about Israel testing God at Massah and Meribah we have also been left with versions of the event as per Biblical Hebrew poetry and those diverge from the narrative plot. I believe that it is the poetic traditions that are the older and more original traditions. According to them, it is God who tested and proved Israel. One of these versions is found, as mentioned above, in Moses's blessing to Levi. The prize of the priesthood, as well as the right to use the Urim and Thumim and offer incense and sacrifices was given to Levi because the tribe withstood the Divine test at Massah and Meribah. The details in this version are also different from the details of the narrative descriptions. While the stories of Massah and Meribah in the Torah revolve around thirst and the lack of water during Israel's wanderings in the desert, a different event is depicted in Levi's blessing; one that involves the sons of Levi's religious loyalty to God (Deut 33:9):

> For they observed your word
> and kept your covenant.

---

[4] This is the way the verb "with whom you contended" should be understood: "who you contended on behalf of, helped Him in his fight". Compare this to Isaiah 1:17 ("plead for the widow").

In other words, the sons of Levi remained loyal to God and His covenant as opposed to those who broke the covenant, apparently by serving other gods. The sons of Levi's zealotry even entailed alienating their closest family (Deut. 32:9):

> who said of his father and mother,
>   'I regard them not';
> he ignored his kin
>   and did not acknowledge his children.

This is indeed devotion worthy of its reward- the right to serve in the holy of places!

Of course, there is a non-negligible similarity between this description and the description of the Levites during the Sin of the Golden Calf (Exodus 32:26–29):

> Then Moses stood in the gate of the camp and said, "Who is on the LORD's side? Come to me!" And all the sons of Levi gathered around him. **27** He said to them, "Thus says the LORD, the God of Israel: Put your sword on your side, each of you! Go back and forth from gate to gate throughout the camp, and each of you kill your brother, your friend, and your neighbor." **28** The sons of Levi did as Moses commanded, and about three thousand of the people fell on that day. **29** Moses said, "Today you have been ordained for the service of the LORD מלאו ידכם ליהו-ה היום)), each one at the cost of a son or a brother, and so have brought a blessing on yourselves this day."

The text describes how the sons of Levi were recruited into a war against those who served the Golden Calf, and how they killed the sinners without discrimination (verses 26–28). In their loyalty to God and the act of purging the camp they overcame their closest family relationships, and it is for this reason that the sons of Levi merited the priesthood (verse 29).[5]

On the other hand, one must recognize the difference between the battle of the sons of Levi as described in the poetry and the one in the narrative. The latter describes an inter-tribal war, in which only the sons of Levi remained loyal to God (Exodus 32:26: "And all the sons of Levi gathered around him"). On the other hand, Levi's blessing (Deut 32:9) mentions only immediate family: father, mother, brother, and son.

---

[5] For the referral of the phrase (מלאו ידיכם)to the priesthood, see Judges 17:5, 12, I Kings 13:33; II Chronicles 13:9.

Meaning the poem describes an inner-tribal religious war among the sons of Levi. To wit, the sin of the Golden Calf is not mentioned in Levi's blessing! In addition, the story of the Golden Calf happens in Sinai while the blessing refers to events at Massah and Meribah. Because of this, commentators have suggested that despite the similarities between them Levi's blessing does not deal with the story of the sin of the Golden Calf.[6]

So, it should be assumed that the poem preserves an ancient tradition, distinct from the story of the Golden Calf, even if some of their details are similar. This tradition revolves around a conflict that occurred at Massah and Meribah within the tribe of Levi, during which those who maintained the covenant fought against those who abandoned it, including their closest family. The catalyst for the conflict was the covenant. Those who clung to it, despite the cost of a conflict with their flesh and blood, as a result merited to serve in the holiest of places, ("they place incense before you/ and whole burnt offerings on your altar"), to consult the Urim and Thumim ("give to Levi your Thummim/ and your Urim to your loyal one"), and to teach law and justice to Israel ("they teach Jacob your ordinances/and Israel your law").[7]

This tradition assumes a covenant between God and the sons of Levi. The covenant demanded loyalty to God alone, a demand which is reflected in the zealous reaction to its breaking. This covenant was made before the conflict within the tribe of Levi at Massah and Meribah.

Now we must inquire as to the time and place of the covenant mentioned in the poetic description. Does the tradition in Moses's Blessing with Levi's blessing teach us about the place where the laws were given, and the covenant was made?[8] By tracking the geographic place marks in the poem we can see that the covenant happened very close to Massah and Meribah.

The order of events is as follows: First God arrived from the region of Sinai and Seir (Deut. 33:2). His journey ended at Massah and Meribah

---

[6] For instance, Loewenstamm (1971); Tigay (2016, vol. II, 824).

[7] The text should read "your laws" תורותיך in plural in keeping with the parallelism, "Your ordinances". This would suit the poem's ancient origins in which the book, the Torah, had not yet been collected and there were still many small priestly teachings being circulated in Israel (see, ibid., Chap. 1).

[8] At the foundation of the description above is the assumption that Moses's Blessing is one coherent composition, as opposed to Seeligmann's opinion, 1964, and others, who contend that the poetic framework of the tribes' blessings is earlier. As mentioned above our assumption regarding the homogeneity of the poem is based on its narrative structure.

(Deut. 33:8) where the covenant was made and then broken by part of the Levites a short time later. It was there that the loyal sons of Levi were chosen to the priesthood for their loyalty.

B

Further support for the reconstruction suggested above can be found in another poetic source, Psalms 81. As scholars have understood through the ages, this psalm is a coherent and early poem that was composed in the Kingdom of Israel before it was destroyed by the Assyrians (ca 720 B.C.).[9] We will focus on the historical description beginning in verse 6. The description starts with slavery in Egypt and Israel's redemption (Psalms 81:6–7).[10] The events after the exodus from Egypt begin in verse 81:8:

> In distress you called, and I rescued you;
> I answered you in the secret place of thunder;
> I tested you at the waters of Meribah. Selah.

[9] The unified nature of the psalm, which is composed of a precise structure in terms of numbers of words and hemistiches, was demonstrated by J Fokkelman, **Major Poems**, vol. III, 143–147. The northern origins of the psalms can be seen in the identification of Israel and Jacob with Jehoseph in the parallelisms in verses 5 and 6. This idea is supported by the mysterious holiday mentioned in verse 4, which describes a tradition unknown from other sources of blowing the shofar at the New Month, and the mysterious "hidden day כסה". See, Gunkel, **Psalms**, on this psalm, as well as Loewenstamm (1958). I do not accept the attempt to date the psalm later, or even to identify within it, a post-Torah influences, or signs of later language. The rare spelling of Jehoseph יהוסף is not a proof, in this case, since it does not negate the basic identification of Joseph and Israel, which is the proof for the northern origin of the psalm. There are no other signs of late language in the psalm, and the extraordinary spelling יהוסף can be explained as an edit, or mistake by a copyist (see Layton 1988 for more on this). The attempt to argue that the psalm was composed post-Torah is not convincing to me. The stylistic similarity of the Torah to this composition is weak (for instance, the description of the exodus from Egypt in verse 11 or the sort-of Torah like language in verses 12–14). Even more so, and as I will explain below, the perspective of the psalm on the question of the origin of the law and the place of the covenant is distinctly different from the perspective of Deuteronomy and the edits that were influenced by it. They establish Horeb as the place where the law was given (So too in the source in Deut. 5–28, and the edit in I Kings 8:9). For the attempt to date this psalm later see Booij (1984b). For the version of the exodus from Egypt in this psalm see for instance Rom-Shiloni (2015).

[10] Loewenstamm (1958) pointed out the Egyptian background of the description in a nice parallel from Egyptian art and the description of the slavery ("your hands were freed from the basket") that depicts a person bearing a basket on his shoulder and holding it from above on his palms.

Despite the parallels, the hemistiches can be internally divided in such a way that shows that this description is referring to two events: The "distress" that God rescued Jehoseph-Israel from, and the answer and test at the waters of Meribah. It seems correct to assume that the "distress" mentioned in the first section of the verse refers to Israel's distress at the Red Sea, where they were pinned between Egypt's army and the sea.[11] God responded with thunder, and split the sea as described in another northern psalm (Psalms 77:19–21):[12]

> The crash of your thunder was in the whirlwind; … Your way was through the sea,/ your path through the mighty waters… You led your people like a flock/ by the hand of Moses and Aaron.

Psalm 81 then describes the test at the waters of Meribah: "I tested you at the waters of Meribah. Selah." The narrative tradition in the Torah establishes that the events at Massah and Meribah happened after the splitting of the sea (Exodus 17:1–7). However, it turns the tables, and in contrast to the psalm, contends that it was Israel that tested God. In addition, the very essence of the test is different in the two sources. While the narrative is concerned with God's presence (is the Lord among us or not?") within the context of water supply, the psalm is concerned with something different, as can be seen in the following verses (Psalms 81:9–11):

> 9 Hear, O my people, while I admonish you; O Israel, if you would but listen to me!
> 10 There shall be no strange god among you; you shall not bow down to a foreign god.
> 11 I am the Lord your God, who brought you up out of the land of Egypt. Open your mouth wide, and I will fill it.

The poet recounts God's demands of His people to not serve other gods. This will be rewarded with abundance. This is, then, is the test that Israel was tested with at the waters of Meribah, according to the psalm.[13]

God's demands in verses 10–11 of the psalms are similar, in their content and text, to the first two of the ten commandments:

---

[11] Compare this to Exodus 14:9, 11 and see Propp (1987, 78); Tate, **Psalms**, vol. II, 323; Hossfeld and Zenger (2005–2011, 324); Goldingay (2006–2008, 552).

[12] In this case as well, its northern origin can be seen in the identification of Joseph with Jacob (Psalms 77:16).

[13] Propp (1987, 57).

Exodus 20:2–4	Psalms 81:10–11
(2) I am the LORD your God, who brought you out of the land of Egypt, out of the house of slavery; you shall have no other gods before me. (3) "You shall not make for yourself an idol, whether in the form of anything that is in heaven above or that is on the earth beneath or that is in the water under the earth. (4) You shall not bow down to them or serve them, for I the LORD your God am a jealous God, punishing children for the iniquity of parents to the third and the fourth generation of those who reject me.	10 There shall be no strange god among you; you shall not bow down to a foreign god. 11 I am the LORD your God, who brought you up out of the land of Egypt. Open your mouth wide, and I will fill it.

The very close similarity of the text, as well as the reversed parallel, a common method of inner quotation in the Hebrew Bible, also known as the "Zeidl principle", indicates a direct relationship between the sources.[14]

In the end, the test described in the psalm ends in failure. Israel commits idolatry at the waters of Meribah and does not keep the covenant that God had made with them just then (Psalms 81:12–13):

> (12) But my people did not listen to my voice;   Israel would not submit to me.
> (13) So I gave them over to their stubborn hearts,   to follow their own counsels.

So, the sequence of events in the psalm can be summarized as follows: after the nation's liberation from slavery in Egypt, God saved them from the distress they found themselves in at the banks of the Red Sea. After crossing the sea, they arrived at the waters of Meribah. It is there that God spoke to the entire nation and issued a command that is very similar in content to the first two of the ten commandments that were given at Sinai according to the Torah narrative. The overarching principle is the prohibition against idolatry. The nation is tested as to whether they will obey this prohibition and are ensured the reward of Divine abundance if they listen to God's commandment: "Open your mouth wide and I will fill it." However, the nation fails the test, serves other gods, and disobeys God's command.

---

[14] Seidel, Parallels. His focus was on Isaiah and Psalms. Later, his method was proven and established in reference to Samuel-Kings and Chronicles as well. Kalimi (2005, 232–274).

C

So, there are two early northern poetic compositions—Moses's Blessings in Deut. 33, and Psalms 81—that reflect a similar tradition, different from the one we are familiar with from the Torah narrative. This tradition establishes that the covenant between God and Israel and its breaking was at the waters of Meribah and not at Sinai-Horeb as in the Torah. Mt. Sinai, which is in Seir-Edom-Midian is God's origin place in the poetic tradition, and it is from there that He goes out to save His people and take them out of Egypt. After the exodus He commands them and makes a covenant with them next to the waters of Meribah. It is difficult to confidently establish the location of the waters of Meribah. However, it is apparently close to the Red Sea, since the date of the revelation and the Divine test in Psalm 81 is mentioned concurrently to the splitting of the sea (Psalms 81:8):

> In distress you called, and I rescued you;
> I answered you in the secret place of thunder;
> I tested you at the waters of Meribah. *Selah.*

Though indeed the poetic sources are not entirely identical, they are in complete agreement regarding the main points that touch on the location and characteristics of verbal revelation, the covenant and its breaking. It seems then that there is one early tradition that is evident in the two northern early poetic sources.

This is to say: There is the narrative tradition in the Torah regarding the revelation, the giving of the commandments, and the making of the covenant at Mt. Sinai, as well as its breaking with the sin of the Golden Calf at the foot of the mountain. The sons of Levi were granted the priesthood for their zealousness in wiping out the sinners at Sinai (Exodus 32:26–29). At the same time, there is an alternative tradition that is preserved in pieces of poetry according to which God did indeed go out from Sinai, however, the giving of the commandments, and the making of the covenant did not happen there, but rather at the waters of Meribah. It was there that the conflict over loyalty to the covenant split families, and possibly led to terrible bloodshed, occurred.[15] At the end of the conflict the loyal sons of

---

[15] Should Deut. 33:9 be read in the spirit of the later texts in Exodus 32:27–29? This is one potential explanation but is not a necessity. It is also possible that it is referring to division and estrangement without killing. See the discussion in Driver (1902, 400–401); Tigay (2016, vol. II, 824–825).

Levi were sanctified to serve in the priesthood because they remained faithful to the covenant at the waters of Meribah. This then reveals a clear and sharp division between the poetry and the Torah narrative regarding the location of the foundational events in the history of Israel: the giving of the commandments and the covenant. According to the Torah narrative these events occurred at Mt. Sinai-Horeb. On the other hand, the early poetic traditions do not attribute any verbal revelation at Mt. Sinai and establish the location of the verbal revelation and the covenant at the waters of Meribah.[16]

BIBLIOGRAPHY

T. Booij, 1984a, "Mountain and Theophany in the Sinai Narrative", *Biblica* 65, 1–26.

T. Booij, 1984b, "The Background of the Oracle in Psalm 81", *Biblica* 65, 465–475.

S.R. Driver, 1902, *Deuteronomy* (ICC) (2nd ed.), Edinburgh.

David N. Freedman, 1980, "The Poetic Structure of the Framework of Deuteronomy 33", in: G.A. Rendsburg et al. (eds.), *The Bible World (Fs. Cyrus H. Gordon)*, New York, 25–46.

J. Goldingay, *Psalms* (Baker Commentary on the Old Testament Wisdom and Psalms), I-III, Ada MI 2006–2008.

F.L. Hossfeld — E. Zenger, *Psalms* (Engl. Ttansl. by L.M. Maloney) (Hermeneia), I-III, Minneapolis 2005–2011.

I. Kalimi, 2005, *The Reshaping of Ancient Israelite History in Chronicles*, Winona Lake IN.

S.C. Layton, 1988, "Jehoseph n Ps 81,6", *Biblica* 69, 406–411.

S.A. Loewenstamm, 1958, "The Bearing of Psalm 81 upon the Problem of Exodus", *EI* 5, 80–82.

S.A. Loewenstamm, 1971, "The Investiture of Levi" (1971), in: idem, From Babylon to Canaan: Studies in the Bible and Its Oriental Background (ed. By Y. Avishur and J. Blau), Jerusalem 1992, 55–65.

W.H.C. Propp, 1987, *Water in the Wilderness* (HSM 68), Atlanta GA.

---

[16] Booij's insights in 1984a, are close in some of its details to my conclusions here. However, his discussion focuses on the two layers in the Torah: the layer of the Mountain of God, Horeb, on the one hand, and the layer of the later Sinai tradition, on the other hand. Our focus, on the other hand is the distinction between early poetry (and the tradition regarding the waters of Meribah that is preserved in them) and the narrative tradition about Sinai-Horeb.

D. Rom-Shiloni, 2015, ""On the day I Took Them out of the Land of Egypt": A Non-Deuteronomic Phrase within Jeremiah's Conception of Covenant", *VT* 65, 621–647.

I.L. Seeligmann, 1964, "A Psalm from Pre-Regal Times", *VT* 14, 75–92.

J.H. Tigay, 2016, Deuteronomy (Mikra Leyisrael), vol. I–II, Tel Aviv.

A. Toeg, 1969, "A Textual Note on 1 Samuel XIV 41", *VT* 19, 493–498.

C. Van Dam, 1997, *The Urim and Thummim: A Means of Revelation in Ancient Israel*, Winona Lake IN.

CHAPTER 7

The Waters of Meribah and the Waters of Marah

A

So, we have established that the text in Psalms 81:9–12 freely quotes from the collection that is known as the Ten Commandments. According to the psalm, these commandments were given at the waters of Meribah and not at Mt. Sinai-Horeb as in the narrative description in the Torah. The poetic description asserts that the nation rebelled at the waters of Meribah and broke the covenant close to its making. This picture is in congruence with the order of events that is evident from Levi's blessing (Deut. 33:8–11). So, it is clear that the early poetic traditions from the northern kingdom were aware of a story about revelation, lawgiving and commandments, the making of a covenant and its breaking. However, as mentioned above, it establishes that the location of these events was at the waters of Meribah and not Mt. Sinai. Though, according to the poems God did appear and came up from Sinai, His seminal communication with Israel happened at a different location and at a different time than that which is described in the narrative. The descriptions in Levi's blessing and Psalms 81, indicate, as mentioned, that the events at the waters of Meribah occurred a short time after the exodus from Egypt and the splitting of the Red Sea.

The story of the waters of Meribah obviously brings to mind the story of the waters of Marah (Exodus 15:22–25) in which the Israelites rebel when there is no water for them to drink a short time after the splitting of the sea. God gives Israel water, laws, and makes a covenant with them:

© The Author(s), under exclusive license to Springer Nature
Switzerland AG 2024
I. Knohl, *Biblical Sinai traditions*,
https://doi.org/10.1007/978-3-031-77983-1_7

Then Moses ordered Israel to set out from the Red Sea, and they went into the wilderness of Shur. They went three days in the wilderness and found no water. **23** When they came to Marah, they could not drink the water of Marah because it was bitter. That is why it was called Marah. **24** And the people complained against Moses, saying, "What shall we drink?" **25** He cried out to the LORD, and the LORD showed him a piece of wood; he threw it into the water, and the water became sweet.

There the LORD[ᶜ] made for them a statute and an ordinance, and there he put them to the test. **26** He said, "If you will listen carefully to the voice of the LORD your God, and do what is right in his sight, and give heed to his commandments and keep all his statutes, I will not bring upon you any of the diseases that I brought upon the Egyptians, for I am the LORD who heals you."The short story before us is similar in many of its details to the tradition in the poems. The period of time is similar to the one in the poetic tradition: three days after crossing the Red Sea, Israel comes to a spring and rebels due to its bitter waters and their distressing thirst. Moses sweetens the waters at God's instructions, and immediately afterwards the nation receives laws and makes a covenant near the spring. At the end the text asserts that it was God who tested Israel at Marah: "There the LORD made for them a statute and an ordinance, and there he put them to the test.". Though the essence of the test is not clear and at first reading is connected to the lack of water, scholars have actually pointed to the restrained promise in the next verse (Exodus 15:26): "If you will listen carefully to the voice of the LORD your God, and do what is right in his sight, and give heed to his commandments and keep all his statutes, I will not bring upon you any of the diseases that I brought upon the Egyptians, for I am the LORD who heals you." Remaining loyal to God and keeping His commandments guarantees a reward and protection against the ailments of Egypt.[1]

---

[1] Compare this to Deut. 7:6–16 (15): "The LORD will turn away from you every illness; all the dread diseases of Egypt that you experienced, he will not inflict on you, but he will lay them on all who hate you." For the background of the covenant and the text in Exodus 15:26, see Propp (1987, 52–53); Propp, **Exodus**, vol. I, 581–582. Scholars have discussed

As mentioned, Moses's Blessings and Psalm 81 have their origins in the cultural legacy of the northern tribes. This too, seems to be true about the tradition regarding the waters of Marah. There are structural similarities between the narrative sequences of the splitting of the Red Sea and the sweetening of the waters of Marah on the one hand, and the splitting of the Jordan and the sweetening of the waters of Jericho by Elijah and Elisha (II Kings 2:1–22), on the other. The close relationship between the texts is evident not only in their order and sequence. The sweetening of the waters of Jericho by Elisha (II Kings 2:19–22) is also similar in its details to the story of the waters of Marah. Both stories describe the process of making a water source fit to drink via methods that resemble magic: in the story in Exodus, it is a piece of wood shown to Moses that makes the water sweet (Exodus 15:25), and in II Kings it is a plate of salt that Elisha flings into the water (II Kings 2:21). The root for the word, healing, *r.p'*, appears in both stories, and in both of them the healing is ascribed to God (Exodus 15:16, II Kings 2:21). There is even an interpretive relationship between the two texts. The connection between the declaration that ends the story of Marah (15, etc. "...I am the Lord who heals you.") and the sweetening of the water that comes before it is unclear. However, the causality between the two events is interpreted and emphasized in Elisha's words (II Kings 2:21): "Thus says the LORD: I have healed this water; from now on neither death nor miscarriage shall come from it."[2]

the close relationship of this text to Deuteronomy and its style. There are those who see the story of the waters of Marah as a late Deuteronomist insertion (for instance, Childs 1974, 267), and see the survey of opinions in Propp's Exodus 574–575). However, the story's style is different than what is customary in Deuteronomist tradition, and there is a place to see it as a part of an early layer in the development of this tradition (called proto-Deuteronomist). (See, Brekelmans 1966, as well as Ausloos's rich survey, 2013). Even if we accept the theory that the story belongs to the later layer in the history of Deuteronomist composition and the creation of the Torah, it is not out of the realm of possibility that it preserves or echoes a relatively ancient tradition. The possibility that ancient passages would pop up at a later stage in the history of the literature and the metamorphosis of the traditions has been demonstrated in a different context by Cassuto, Israelite Epic. This possibility is supported in this case by the exceptional character of the giving of the laws at Marah in its divergence from the Sinai-Horeb tradition which dominates the Torah in general, and Deuteronomy in specific,. The singular nature of the story indicates that it preserves an early and independent tradition. For the status of scholarship on the story of Marah see German (2013).

[2] On the affinity between the story of Marah and the story of Elisha and the waters of Jericho, see Zakovitch (1991, 75–76). He points to additional connections and parallels between the stories of Elijah and Elisha and the tradition of the exodus from Egypt and the figure of Moses (ibid., 69–79). On the consolidation of the tradition regarding Moses and its affinity to the consolidation of the stories of Elijah and Elisha and northern prophetic

The substantial similarities between the two stories and their narrative surroundings, to the point that it appears that they were designed in each other's image, proves that they were composed in the same environment. The northern origin of the traditions regarding Elijah and Elisha indicates then, that the story of Marah was created in a similar milieu.[3] So the story of Marah is another echo of the northern tradition reconstructed from the pieces of poetry about the giving of law, and the covenant and its breaking at the waters of Meribah. It metamorphosized and was placed among the Torah traditions about Israel's complaints during their wanderings in the desert.

B

Levi's blessing, Psalm 81, and the story of the waters of Marah have a joint foundation, unique to them. It is only in these texts that God tests the nation (or the sons of Levi) near the water as to whether they will keep His

---

circles, see Rofé (1988, 2–16) who wrote following M. Buber. Though my student Tzemach Yoreh (2010, 201–203) attributes the kernel of the story of Marah to a northern source E, he ascribes a large portion of the short story to the Judean adaption by J. In a previous study he expresses doubts regarding the affinity between the northern source and the stories of the prophets in Kings as proof of the northern origin of E (Yoreh 2003, 237, on).

[3] The number of scholarly voices that contend that the composition of the stories of the prophets and their integration into the Book of Kings was later, has grown. Those who hold this opinion attribute much of this material, and specifically the traditions regarding Elijah, to the post Deuteronomistic stage in the creation of the Book of Kings, which is dated, at the earliest to the first days of the return to Zion (see, for instance, McKenzie 1991, 81–100, and his new Commentary: Mckenzie 2019, as well as Susanne Otto 2003). This opinion had its followers as far back as classical scholarship, see for instance Steuernagel (1912, 359ff., esp. 369–379). I believe that the stories of the prophets were created and developed orally in the geographical and historical environment in which those prophets were active in, thus, in the Kingdom of Israel between the ninth and eighth centuries B.C.E. With the expansion of literacy in the north at the beginning of the eighth century the process of writing those traditions down began, though we cannot negate the possibility of the integration of later material to these traditions, from the period after the fall of Samaria, I believe that the main collections of the stories regarding the northern prophets were created before the destruction of the Kingdom of Israel in which the important status of these heroes were known. Another aspect that gives credence to this source of the creation of the prophetic narratives

laws or not. In the rest of the traditions regarding the rebellions in the desert and a lack of water, it is the nation who tests God![4]

It is possible that this unique thread shows up in another source that has an affinity to the northern tribes.[5] The speech in Jeremiah 7:21–28 reflects a unique and revolutionary worldview. Verses 21–22 express the rejection of the established ritual order as well as the historical and religious ideas inherent in them:

is the revolution of prophecy that occurred in Israel over the course of the eighth century B.C.E. The figures of miracle workers like Elijah and Elisha were pushed aside in favor of the written prophets, regarding whom almost no similar stories of miracles were preserved. It is hard to imagine how those types of stories would bloom in the spiritual realities of those later generations, in which the status of prophets like Elijah and Elisha were not preserved. In addition, the consolidation of the stories regarding the wonders done by prophets naturally occurred in the circles of their admirers, in the same way that the Gospels were created, and, vastly different, the Hasidic stories like "the praises of the Baal Shem Tov". These conditions which are necessary for the creation of stories of prophets were destroyed after the horrors that were visited upon the northern kingdom during the Assyrian invasion of 732–734 and remained destroyed until the destruction of Samaria in about 720 BCE. The expulsion of a great portion of the kingdom's population and the material poverty that the Assyrian invasion brought with it essentially led to the end of the physical and social existence of the followers of Elijah and Elisha (the sons of the prophets). It seems that the written traditions created by these circles found their way to Judah via refugees from Samaria, though it is difficult to imagine the living continuation of the circles of followers of the northern prophets after the fall of Samaria or in the Babylonian exile. Therefore, I accept the opinion that the prophetic narratives in the Book of Kings preserves early northern traditions. For this opinion see, Rofé (1988, 3–85). (regarding the stories of Elisha; though he (ibid., 161–171) establishes the composition of the stories of Elijah at the time of Manasseh he still acknowledges that there are early passages within the stories). See also Lemaire (1990, 1991).

[4] For instance, Numbers 20:1–13; Deuteronomy 9:24; Psalms 85:9.

[5] Jeremiah the Prophet came from Benjaminite territory, a boundary zone between Judah and Israel which changed hands between kingdoms. This area, then, was a melting pot for northern and southern traditions and helped mediate between the sister cultures; this has been demonstrated from various angles by: Knauf (2006); Davies (2007); Na'aman (2009). Compare this also too Amos the Prophet who was from Tekoa in Judah, but was active in Beit El, the royal temple of the northern kingdom. Jeremiah's connection to northern culture is evident in, among other things, the affinity his prophecies have with the prophecies of Hosea (Gross 1931; Weinfeld 1972, 366–370).

> Thus says the LORD of hosts, the God of Israel: Add your burnt
> offerings to your sacrifices, and eat the flesh. **22** For in the day that
> I brought your ancestors out of the land of Egypt, I did not speak to
> them or command them concerning burnt offerings and sacrifices.

The prophet expropriates the sanctity of the burnt offerings, which
are forbidden to eat (Lev. 1:3–13) and counts them among the sacrifices which are permitted to eat. He justifies the secularization of
burnt offerings with the assertion that God did not actually command His people to sacrifice when they left Egypt (verse 21): "For
in the day that I brought your ancestors out of the land of Egypt, I
did not speak to them or command them concerning burnt offerings
and sacrifices."[6]

The rest of the speech describes the content of the covenant that God
did make with Israel during the exodus from Egypt (Jeremiah 7:23): "But
this command I gave them, "Obey my voice, and I will be your God, and
you shall be my people; walk only in the way that I command you, so that
it may be well with you." The prophet establishes that at the exodus a
covenant was established between God and the people that conditions
that the good of the people on loyalty to God and His ways. This covenant
was broken the moment it was made, and remained broken throughout all
the generations that followed up until the time of the prophet (verses
24–25):

> Yet they did not obey or incline their ear, but, in the stubbornness of
> their evil will, they walked in their own counsels and looked back-
> ward rather than forward. **25** From the day that your ancestors came
> out of the land of Egypt until this day, I have persistently sent all my
> servants the prophets to them, day after day.

---

[6] In the negation of the tradition regarding the source of the sacrifices worship in the commandments that were given during the exodus from Egypt, Jeremiah resembles to two other
northern prophets. Compare this to Amos 5:25, Hosea 3:4. On the revolutionary character
of this negation see Weinfeld (1976, 52ff).

The content and style of Jeremiah's speech are similar to and maybe even echo, Psalms 81:9–13:

Psalms 81:9–13	*Jeremiah 7:24–25*
9 There shall be no strange god among you; you shall not bow down to a foreign god. 10 I am the LORD your God, who brought you up out of the land of Egypt. Open your mouth wide, and I will fill it. 11 "But my people did not listen to my voice; Israel would not submit to me. 12 So I gave them over to their stubborn hearts, to follow their own counsels. 13 O that my people would listen to me, that Israel would walk in my ways!	24 Yet they did not obey or incline their ear, but, in the stubbornness of their evil will, they walked in their own counsels and looked backward rather than forward. 25 From the day that your ancestors came out of the land of Egypt until this day, I have persistently sent all my servants the prophets to them, day after day.

The two texts describe the breaking of the covenant and Israel's rebellion with similar, and even identical phrases: "followed their own counsels", "their stubborn hearts", and "they did not listen."

Their reversed order could indicate a direct connection as a parallel chiastic quotation, known as the "Seidl Principle".

Whether this is a direct quotation or a more liberal echo, the two sources are in accord on one subject: immediately after the exodus from Egypt a covenant was made between God and His nation and was thereafter broken, apparently through disloyalty and idolatry. It seems then, that the speech in Jeremiah 7 is another echo of the ancient northern poetic tradition, just like the echo in the Marah story in Exodus 15.

C

To sum up our current findings: We have reconstructed an independent tradition regarding the giving of laws and the breaking of the covenant at the waters of Meribah from the traces that were preserved in ancient northern poetry such as Moses's blessing to Levi (Deut. 33), and Psalm 81. Now we have found that this tradition also left traces in pieces of narrative (the story of the waters of Marah) and prophecy (Jeremiah 7). Thes two last soutces also have an affinity to the cultural legacy of the northern kingdom. All the sources describe the covenant and the giving of the commandments and their breaking on the way from Egypt to Canaan.

However, unlike the primary tradition in the Torah, which establishes the location of these events at Mt. Sinai, the northern tradition establishes them at another place, close to Egypt and the Red Sea, and near a source of water, either the waters of Meribah or the waters of Marah. This landmark is either clearly noted (in Levi's blessing, Psalms 81, and the story of the waters of Marah), or is apparent from the source's silence regarding Sinai (Jeremiah 7).

We will soon see that this tradition is also different in terms of the covenant itself. Unlike in the Sinai tradition, Moses does not play a central role in the covenant. Though he is a central figure in the story of Marah, the covenant between God and His nation is made directly, without Moses as an intermediary. This is also the case in the rest of the sources that have preserved the memory of this tradition. The fragmented and fragile character of the northern tradition, the tradition of the spring, is indicative of its marginality relative to the Sinai tradition, and perhaps even indicates that it was pushed aside.

Now we must ask: what is the framework for the creation of the northern tradition, and what is its relationship to the Sinai tradition; how was it pushed aside for the tradition of the mountain, which is the primary one in the Torah, and which was accepted and sanctified in Israelite tradition for generations to come.

BIBLIOGRAPHY

H. Ausloos, 2013, "The 'Proto-Deuteronomist': Fifty Years Later", *OTE* 26, 531–558.

C. Brekelmans, 1966, "Die sogenanten deuteronomistischen Elemente in Gen. bis Num.: Ein Beitrag zur Vorgeschichte des Deuteronomiums", *SVT* 15, 90–96.

B.S. Childs, 1974, *Exodus* (OTL), London.

P.R. Davies, 2007, "The Trouble with Benjamin", in: R. Rezetko et al. (eds.), *Reflection and Refraction (Fs. A.G. Auld)* (SVT 113), Leiden, 93–111.

B.T. German, 2013, "Moses at Marah", *VT* 63, 47–58.

K. Gross, 1931, "Hoseas Einfluss auf Jeremias Anschauungen", *NKZ* 42, 241–255, 327–343.

E.A. Knauf, 2006, "Bethel: The Israelite Impact on Judean Language and Literature", in: O. Lipschits and M. Oeming (ed.), *Judah and the Judeans in the Persian Period*, Winona Lake IN, 291–350.

A. Lemaire, 1990, "Joas, roi d'Israël, et la première rédaction du cycle d'Élisée", in:C. Brekelmans and J. Lust (eds.), *Pentateuchal and Deuteronomistic Studies; Papers Read at the XIIIth IOSOT Congress, Leuven, 1989*, Leuven, 245–254.

A. Lemaire, 1991, "Géhazi et les "hauts faits d'Élisée" : remarques sur l'histoire de la rédaction des cycles d'Élie et d'Élisée", in: J.J. Adler (ed.), *Haim M.I. Gevaryahu Memorial Volume*, I-II, Jerusalem, II, 41–52.

S.L. Mckenzie, 1991, *The Trouble with Kings: The Composition of the Book of Kings in the Deuteronomistic History* (SVT 42), Leiden.

S.L. Mckenzie, 2019, 1 Kings 16 - 2 Kings 16 (IECOT), Stuttgart.

N. Na'aman, 2009, "Saul, Benjamin and the Emergence of 'Biblical Israel'", *ZAW* 121, 211–224, 335–349.

Susanne Otto, 2003, "The Composition of the Elijah-Elisha Stories and the Deuteronomistic History", *JSOT* 27, 487–508.

W.H.C. Propp, 1987, *Water in the Wilderness* (HSM 68), Atlanta GA.

A. Rofé, 1988, *The Prophetical Stories: The Narratives About the Prophets in the Hebrew Bible, Their Literary Types and History*, Jerusalem.

C. Steuernagel, 1912, *Einleitung in das Alte Testament*, Tübingen.

M. Weinfeld, 1972, *Deuteronomy and the Deuteronomic School*, Oxford.

M. Weinfeld, 1976, "Jeremiah and the Spiritual Metamorphosis of Israel", *ZAW* 88, 17–56.

T. Yoreh, 2003, *The Elohistic Source: Its Structure and Unity* (unpublished Dissertation; The Hebrew University), Jerusalem [in Hebrew].

T.L. Yoreh, 2010, *The First Book of God* (BZAW 402), Berlin.

Y. Zakovitch, 1991, *"And You Shall Tell Your Son…": The Concept of Exodus in the Bible*, Jerusalem.

CHAPTER 8

The Tradition of the Spring, the Tradition of the Mountain and the Beginning of Literacy in the Northern Kingdom

A

Earlier in our discussion we demonstrated that there are additional traces of the tradition of the giving of the commandments and the making of the covenant near the water beyond the fragments found in early poetry. Once again, the question must be asked: what is the relationship between this tradition and the narrative tradition in the Torah, according to which these events took place at Mt. Sinai? These two traditions are distinguished from one another not only in their content but also in the way they were preserved. While the Sinai tradition was preserved coherently and sequentially, and is the dominant story in the Torah, the tradition of the spring was preserved in fragments and traces, like tiny pieces of a mosaic. Does this distinction stem from the differing origins of the traditions, one from the north and the other from Judah? Maybe, in keeping with this theory, the northern tradition was pushed aside for the southern Sinai tradition, and it is for this reason that its remnants are a piecemeal that survived the winnowing carried out by Judean scribes.

Attributing the traditions to Judah and Israel, respectively is a tempting solution. The descriptions of the making of the covenant and its breaking at Meribah or Marah are all connected, in one way or another to the northern heritage embedded in the Hebrew Bible. The attribution of this tradition to the northern tribes suits the broken and fragile character of northern tradition. It befits the horrors that were visited upon the north

© The Author(s), under exclusive license to Springer Nature
Switzerland AG 2024
I. Knohl, *Biblical Sinai traditions*,
https://doi.org/10.1007/978-3-031-77983-1_8

and the rushed and battered way in which the cultural legacy of the north moved south, fleeing from the occupying Assyrian army. In contrast, the continuous and complete character of the Sinai tradition, on the face of it, suits its attribution to Judah. Despite the destruction and exile to Babylon that was visited on Judean society, it remained relatively unified and consolidated even in exile. So, naturally, the Judeans were able to preserve their legacy more completely than the northern tribes who were scattered to the wind. In addition, according to this explanation, the strength and centrality of the Jewish-Babylonian immigration to Judah during the return to Zion is nicely congruent with the centrality of the Sinai tradition in the Torah. It is this tradition that vanquished differing traditions such as the northern tradition of the spring.

However, a close investigation and comparison between the two traditions raises doubts regarding this solution. As you may remember, the remnants of the spring tradition were assembled from Moses's blessing to Levi (Deut. 33:8–11), and Psalms 81. Other reflections of this tradition were found in the story of Marah (Exodus 15:23–26) and Jeremiah's speech in Jeremiah 7:21–16. The poetic sources are clearly northern. The tribe of Judah has a marginal place in Moses's Blessings (Deut. 33:7). The remaining southern tribe, Simeon, isn't mentioned at all in the poem. On the other hand, the children of Joseph have a prominent place in the blessing and are described as strong and influential (Deut. 33:13–17). Their glorification in the face of the marginalization of the southern tribes indicates that this poem is northern in origin. Psalm 81 identifies Jacob and Israel with Jehoseph. Clearly this identification could only occur among the children of Joseph and the northern tribes. It has no natural place among Jerusalemite compositions.

The northern connection is also evident in the remnants of this tradition in narrative and prophecy. The Marah story (Exodus 15:23–26) has clear affinities in its content and context to the series of stories about Elijah and Elisha from the north. This is the case regarding the echo of the tradition of the spring in Jeremiah's prophecy (Jeremiah 7:21–26) as well. The prophet was descended from the priests of Shiloh, and was from Anatot in Benjamin, a region on the seam between north and south and a place of transition and meeting between the cultures of the two sister kingdoms. Thus, all the examples of the tradition of the giving of laws and the making of the covenant and its breaking next to the spring are from sources about which there is a good reason to believe that they are northern in origin.

The Sinai tradition, which establishes that God's revelation, the giving of the law, the making of the covenant and its breaking occurred at the mountain is concentrated in Exodus 19–34. It appears once again, as a review in Deut. 4–10. However, a close look at this tradition in the Book of Exodus shows that it too has northern elements. The most prominent of them is the Sin of the Golden Calf in Exodus 32. As is well-known, the story and figure of Aharon has a deep affinity with the figure and actions of Jeroboam the son of Nebat and his ritual "reforms" in the northern kingdom in the Book of Kings: The children of Aharon and Jeroboam have identical names, Nadab and Abiah-Abihu, and identical ends: an unnatural death in their youth (Leviticus 10:1–2, I Kings 14:1–18, 15:25–31). Both Aharon and Jeroboam created calves in a similar way (Exodus 32:1–3, I Kings 12:28), and declared: "These are your gods, O Israel, who brought you up out of the land of Egypt!" (Exodus 32:4, I Kings 12:28). Both of them even established a holiday involving the worship of the calves (Exodus 32:5, I Kings 12:32).[1]

Another northern element in the story of the Golden Calf in the Book of Exodus is the central role and positive description of Joshua the son of Nun. The Ephraimite hero appears as Moses's close attendant and companion. These characteristics of Joshua appear throughout the story (Exodus 24:13, 32:17, 33:11).[2] Though the figure of Joshua was later absorbed into southern circles, it seems that his original roots are in the tribe of Ephraim.

Though the tradition of the mountain cannot be completely attributed to the north, it contains a non-negligible number of artifacts from the legacy of the north. It seems then that the distinction between it and the

---

[1] The primary discussion regarding the similarities between Aharon and Jeroboam and the descriptions of the calves in both sources can be found in Aberbach and Smolar (1967). They counted no less than 13 similarities between them! It is also possible that these similarities are not limited to the polemic layer which is interested in the calves and their makers. There are scholars who identify an earlier layer in the story, in which there is a positive tradition about the making of the calf, similar to the traditions regarding the foundation of the rites and the creation of ritual accruement such as the building of the tabernacle and the establishment of temples in the ancient Near-East. See, Hurowitz (1983); Chung (2010, 47–50). I am not convinced of the existence of such a layer in the story in the Torah. In any case, that it is very likely that there was an alternative story that existed among the priests of Beit El that described the creation of the calf in a positive light.

[2] On the northern origin of the traditions regarding Joshua see Rofé (2004), Farber (2016, 86–140).

tradition of the covenant at the spring cannot be based on their different origins: Ephraim as opposed to Judah. The source of the difference between them must be sought in a different context.

B

I believe that the difference between the traditions should be sought, first and foremost, in the differences between poetic composition and written composition. Most of the expressions of the tradition of the spring are poetic. The story of Marah is an exceptional representation of the poetic tradition in narrative form. On the other hand, the tradition of the making of the covenant at Sinai in Exodus 19–34 is a characteristic example of prose. This is also the case in terms of its appearance in Deuteronomy 4–10.[3]

As we discussed in Chap. 1, archeological scholarship shows that knowledge of literacy in Israel and Judah was quite limited before the eighth century BCE.[4] Of course, one must take into account the fact that the preservability of writing is limited by the perishable character of the writing materials used in Israel, such as parchment and papyrus. So, we must qualify our words in recognition of the fact that we do not have the whole picture, but rather what we see is the result of random archeological findings. Even though, the eighth century BCE was probably a turning point in terms of the scope of literacy and written works found in Israel—first in the north and then in the south. Up until then the art of writing was limited to the educated elite in temples and royal courts. Naturally, the number of narrative works- as opposed to administrative- was limited. Israelite culture was primarily oral.

As mentioned, there is a consistent rise in the number of written findings in the kingdom of Israel beginning from the latter part of the ninth century and the beginning of the eighth century BCE. These include well-known artifacts such as the Samaria Ostraca and the Kuntillet Ajrud inscription which contain both sacred and secular writing. Over the course of the eighth century written findings in the kingdom of Judah also increased. Congruently Hebrew Biblical composition changed as well. During this period the written prophets first appeared- first in the north (Amos and Hosea) and then later in Judah (Isaiah the son of Amoz and

---

[3] The story of the creation of the Golden Calf at Horeb is also represented in poetry in Psalm 106:19–33, but this is a late psalm based on Torah stories.
[4] I am repeating, in short, what I said in Chap. 1. For another look into the rise of literacy in Israel, starting in the north, and afterwards in Judah, see Finkelstein (2020).

Micah). The prophecies of their predecessors, Elijah and Elisha, were not preserved, and the memories of their personalities and deeds were transmitted by word of mouth (II Kings 8:4). The expansion of writing and the creation of the community of readers is, it seems, one of the reasons for this change.

I believe that the transition from the tradition of the giving of the law and the covenant near the water, which is primarily poetic, to the tradition of the giving of the Torah at Sinai, which is prose, is related to the change that I described. The tradition of the spring was created before the rise of literacy during the eighth century BCE, at the height of the days of oral poetry. On the other hand, the tradition of the mountain is an expression of the genesis of the Hebrew Biblical narrative and the rise of literary culture in Israel.[5]

A certain confirmation of this idea can be found in the Sin of the Golden Calf which is a part of the tradition of the mountain. It is possible to establish the historical background for the denunciation of the calf in the story in Exodus 32 with some measure of certainty. This can serve as a relatively stable "chronological anchor" for establishing the relationships between the traditions.

The sources that we have indicate that worship of the calf was a central and accepted ritual in the kingdom of Israel throughout its entire existence. It was considered a legitimate type of worship of God, and even those zealous for God did not find fault in it. There is no hint of the denunciation of the "sin of Jeroboam" and the calves in the stories of Elijah and Elisha or in the prophecies of Amos. These latter, Elisha and Amos even visited Beit El (see, for instance II Kings 2:23, Amos 7:12–17), but did not comment on the calf standing in the royal temple of the north. Even when King Jehu destroyed the House of Ahab and eradicated the worship of Baal from Israel (II Kings 9–10) he did not touch the calves.[6]

---

[5] Regarding the literary character of the Sinai tradition, and specifically the text in Exodus 24, see Schniedewind (2004, 121–134).

[6] Even so, this doesn't prevent the text from describing him as zealous of behalf God (II Kings 10:15–17). There is a clear dichotomy in the relationship of the editor of the Book of Kings to Jehu and his house. Their close and warm relationships with the prophets of God are described in detail (9:1–10, 13:14–19, 14:25–26) and the few points of positive appreciation of the north and its rulers are concentrated in the description of the history of this dynasty (10:28, 30; 13:4–5, 22–25; 15:12). On the other hand, the text is quick to qualify the positive aspects of the figures of Jehu and his house and accuses them of sticking to "Jeroboam's sin" and worship of the calf (10:29, 31; 13:2–3, 6, 11; 14:24). The secondary

Worship of the calves is first rejected in the prophecies of Hosea in the waning years of the kingdom of Israel. He spurns the calf as a Divine symbol, disparages it as a hewn idol, and denounces its worship harshly (Hosea 8:4–6, 10:5–8). He looks forward to a time when the calf would be destroyed: "For it is from Israel /an artisan made it;/it is not God./The calf of Samaria/ shall be broken to pieces." This rejection continues in the final edition of the Book of Kings. The editor denounces the establishment of the calves by Jeroboam the son of Nebat (I Kings 12:26–30) and sees "Jeroboam's sin" as the primary cause of the fall of Samaria and the exile of the ten tribes (II Kings 17:21–23). This stage in the polemic against the calves occurred between the fall of Samaria and the destruction of Jerusalem.[7]

It seems then that the condemnation of the Golden Calf in Exodus 32 can serve as chronological anchor for the creation of the tradition of the covenant and the giving of the law at Sinai. It can be assumed that the first layer of this tradition was created as early as the last days of the kingdom of Israel. This fits the characteristics of the tradition as a sophisticated narrative composition dependent on a developed culture of literacy. It was

characteristics of at least some of those qualifications is clear. There is reason to assume then, that at the foundation of the texts about Jehu and his house are positive descriptions, pre-Deuteronomistic, the origins of which are apparently in the courts of the kings in Samaria, as is the opinion of Campbell (1986, 17–124); Lemaire (1990, 1991), and Rofé (2014, 64–71). The subject of northern sources, especially from the days of Jeroboam II, was also the focus of the third edition of *HeBAI* 6 (2017). It seems that in these sources worship of the calves was not a fault, and they were considered legitimate worship of God. It is their secondary adaptations that reject this act and denounce Jehu and his house for continuing in "Jeroboam's Sin". Perhaps it is not for nothing that Jehu's partner in getting rid of the Baal was Jonadab the son of Rechab (II Kings 12:15–17). Apparently, he was Kenite in origin (I Chronicles 2:55). The memory of him as someone was loyal to God and a purist was retained many generations later (Jeremiah 35). (See, ibid., Chap. 3 about the Kenite theory regarding the origins of the Israelite God). Regarding the relationship of Jehu to the calf, see also, Rabbi Judah Halevi, The Kuzari, 4:14.

[7]The opinion that the first stage in the creation of the Book of Kings occurred in the courts of King Hezekiah is tenable. The condemnation of Jeroboam's deeds and the calves at Beit El and Dan also developed there. The influence of Hosea's prophecies is evident in this composition, and there is room to believe that it was the northern scribes who were absorbed into Jerusalem who were behind it (Weippert 1972; Campbell 1986, 125ff.; Rofé 1988, 78–80).

preceded by the tradition of the covenant by the water, which does not mention the sin of the Golden Calf, and which is fundamentally an oral poetic tradition. We must further clarify whether and how the combination of the two processes- the expansion of literacy on the one hand, and the rejection of the rites of the calf, on the other hand- led to the abandonment of the ancient poetic tradition in the northern kingdom.

BIBLIOGRAPHY

M. Aberbach and L. Smolar, 1967, "Aaron, Jeroboam and the Golden Calves", *JBL* 86, 129–140.

A.F. Campbell, 1986, *Of Prophets and Kings: A Late Ninth-Century Document (1 Samuel 1-2 Kings 10)* (CBQMS 17), Washington DC.

Y.H. Chung, 2010, *The Sin of the Calf: The Rise of the Bible's Negative Attitude Toward the Golden Calf*, London — New York.

Z. Farber, 2016, *Images of Joshua in the Bible and its reception* (BZAW 457), Berlin.

Israel Finkelstein, 2020, "The Emergence and Dissemination of Writing in Judah", *Semitica et Classica* 13, 269–282.

A.V. Hurowitz, 1983, "The Golden Calf and the Tabernacle", *Shnaton* 7–8, 51–59 [in Hebrew].

A. Lemaire, 1990, "Joas, roi d'Israël, et la première rédaction du cycle d'Élisée", in:C. Brekelmans and J. Lust (eds.), *Pentateuchal and Deuteronomistic Studies; Papers Read at the XIIIth IOSOT Congress*, Leuven, 1989, Leuven, 245–254.

A. Lemaire, 1991, "Géhazi et les "hauts faits d'Élisée" : remarques sur l'histoire de la rédaction des cycles d'Élie et d'Élisée", in: J.J. Adler (ed.), *Haim M.I. Gevaryahu Memorial Volume*, I-II, Jerusalem, II, 41–52.

A. Rofé, 2004, "Joshua Son of Nun in the History of Biblical Tradition", *Tarbiz* 73, 333–364 [in Hebrew].

A. Rofé, 2014, *The Stories of the Prophets*, [Heb.], Jerusalem.

W.M. Schniedewind, 2004, *How the Bible Became a Book: The Textualization of Ancient Israel*, Cambridge.

H. Weippert, 1972, "Die 'deuteronomistischen' Beurteilungen der Könige von Israel und Juda und das Problem der Redaktion der Königsbücher", *Biblica* 53, 301–339.

CHAPTER 9

The Northern Author and the Book of the Covenant

A

Our investigation has indicated the middle of the eighth century as the assumed date for the transition between the tradition of the revelation and the covenant near the water and the Sinai tradition. We have additionally suggested that this turning point is one expression of the wider social and technological development that was the expansion of literacy and the transition from oral composition and an oral society to written composition and a literate society. In addition, we have suggested that the transition from the tradition of the water to the tradition of the mountain entailed reservations regarding the worship of the calves in the kingdom of Israel and the rejection of these rites, as is reflected in the prophecies of Hosea, the Book of Kings, and the story of the Golden Calf in Exodus 32-34.

As we will discuss below the social and religious worldviews of some of the sources fit this historical context well. It was in the first half of the eighth century BCE that the northern kingdom became stronger and expanded. During the reigns of the kings Jehoahaz and Joash (II Kings 13: 3-5, 14-19), the kingdom succeeded in freeing itself from the yoke of the Arameans. Later, during the reign of Jeroboam II, it even expanded and conquered territory beyond the Jordan in the Bashan and the Golan

I. Knohl, *Biblical Sinai traditions*, https://doi.org/10.1007/978-3-031-77983-1_9

Heights (14:25-27).[1] The new-found power of the northern kingdom came with economic growth and along with it, classism, and social polarization. The administrative and military class became rich as a result of the rising power of the government and its conquests, while the poor farmers became impoverished and were forced to sell their land and even themselves as slaves. This reality echoes in Amos's prophecies, which condemn the corruption and degradation that spread through the Israelite elite as well as the exploitation and suppression of the poor (Amos 2:6-12, 3:9-10, 15; 4:1; 5:18; :1-8, 8:4-6). As if in contradiction to this behavior, Amos describes the religious devotion of the ruling class in Israel, who were punctilious in matters of ritual, and strict about visiting the sanctuary, bringing sacrifices, and celebrating the holidays (Amos 4:4-5; 5:4-5, 21-24;8:4-6). Amos entirely rejects these religious behaviors, which were not accompanied by morality and justice. He denies the value of sacrifices, as well as the fact of their requirement during the wanderings in the desert (Amos 5:21-27). Amos even prophecies the total destruction of the Kingdom of the North and its temples, even though their establishment is attributed to the forefathers of Israel (Amos 5:4-6,26-27;7:7-9). The climax of his words is the direct conflict between the prophet and Amaziah the priest of Beit El, the royal temple (Amos 7:1-17).

The author of the core of the Sinai story in Exodus 19-33—that is to say—the northern author, has some similar opinions to those expressed by Amos.[2] His position can be distilled from the narrative framework that he created as well as the adaptation that he layered on top of the Book of the Covenant (Exodus 20-24). Scholars have discussed the affinity between the narrative framework and the adaptation of the laws in the Book of the Covenant, and it is from these sources that we can begin to understand the

[1] Our knowledge of Jeroboam II's accomplishments are independently confirmed in slight references in the prophecies of Amos (Amos 6:13-14). The growing strength of the kingdom of Israel, among other things, at the expense of the Arameans, was possible also thanks to the weakening of the Assyrians due to internal battles. Assyriah's attention was turned to internal discord and not battle campaigns westward. This allowed for local powers in the west, such as Israel to become stronger and reinforce themselves until the return of the Assyrian battle campaigns during the days of Tiglath Pileser III in the last third of the eighth century BCE. The northern kingdom's freedom from the yoke of the Arameans and its expansion and growth during the period afterwards have left an archaeological footprint. See Finkelstein (2013, 119–140).

[2] As we theorized above, it seems that this author was active in the northern kingdom around the middle of the eighth century BCE. If this is true, he and Amos were close in both location and time.

complicated relationship between the worldviews of the northern author and those expressed in Amos's prophecies.

Unlike Amos, the northern author does not entirely reject the ritual rites. However, he does advocate for simple rites, without fancy artifacts (Exodus 20:22-26).[3] His rites have no place in them for silver and golden idols (Exodus 20:2) and requires only an earthen altar ("You need make for me only an altar of earth" [verse 21]). The author forbids the making of altars from hewn stone, and only allows their construction from unchiseled stones of the field (verse 22).[4] His ritual regulations emphasize that sacrificial worship can be done everywhere, without the need for glorious temples (verse 19-33). As far as he's concerned there is no need for an established priesthood. All of Israel is "a priestly kingdom" (Exodus19:6), a "people consecrated to me", and so everyone is worthy to serve in the holiest of places, without punctiliousness about their priestly heritage.[5]

At the same time, the northern author of the Sinai story shares Amos's moral and social views. There are a few cases of similarities between Amos's admonitions and the regulations established by the northern author-legislator. In general, as will become clear, it seems that this author aspired

[3] Tigay (2004), proved that the unit in Exodus 22-26 is unified in its design and content, and there is no real reason to divide it into strata.

[4] Olyan (1996), theorized that the prohibition against hewn stone stems from ideas of holiness and wholeness, which perceives the processing of the stone as the desecration and invalidation of the stone's ability serve in worship of God (similarly to the Red Heifer which served no purpose other than being sacrificed and burned to be used in contexts of purity). However, Olyan's theory doesn't take into account that this prohibition as well the allowance of collected stones to be used to build an altar is derived from the primary instruction regarding building an earthen altar. Meaning, the issues of wholeness and purity are not the main point.

[5] See also the ritual service of Israelite youth during the covenant ceremony (Exodus 24:5, we will discuss this in depth below). Compare this too to the opinion of Hosea, another northern prophet, who rejects the rites and the priesthood as one, as well as the monarchy (Hosea 3:4), see most recently Knohl (2023). Regarding the rejection of the worship of idols in Exodus 20 and its similarities to the prophecies of Hosea and the polemics against the calves see, Feder (2013). He also discusses the relatively early character of the passage in Exodus 20: 18-22, relative to the later passage that it is similar to in Deuteronomy 4 (ibid., 266–272). In general, I do not accept the widespread trend in today's scholarship to attribute the text in Exodus, or the lion's share of it to later post-Torah editing. On this subject see the various opinions in Blenkinsopp (1999), and Van Seters (1999).

to put right the religious and moral crises of his generation through legislation and regulation.[6]

B

To better appreciate the northern author's composition and positions, as well as their relationship to the prophecies of Amos, we will summarize the history of the law in Israel previous to his activities. What was the nature of the laws such as the ones that are hinted to in the poetic tradition regarding the covenant by the water before the northern author?

We previously looked at Moses's blessing to Levi (Deut. 33:8-11) and the tradition it preserves regarding the events of Massah and Meribah. As you may remember, the priesthood was given to the children of Levi as a reward for their zealous loyalty to God after His revelation during those events. The poem establishes the role of the priesthood as following (verse 10):

> They teach Jacob your ordinances
>   and Israel your law;
> they place incense before you
>   and whole burnt offerings on your altar.

The Levite priests were given the job of bringing sacrifices and teaching the nation God's laws and ordinances.[7] This tradition is in keeping with our additional knowledge of the priests as responsible for teaching the nation to fear God (Deut. 21:5; 24:8; II Kings 17:38; Haggai 2:1-14). From the content of the text, including the adaptation of the text in Levi's blessing, it seems that תורתך, "your law" here is not referring to one established creation known and recognized as the "Torah", but rather, many priestly teachings that were composed and transmitted in priestly circles in Israel over the course of many generations, for almost as long as the existence of temples and established ritual in Israel. These teachings were,

---

[6] Chavel (2015, 197–201) points to the affinity between the northern author's work and the admonitions of Hosea and Amos and the reality of the second half of the eighth century BCE in Israel.

[7] It seems that the text should be amended and read in plural "teachings" to suit the parallel to "laws" as it is preserved in the Samarian version. As we saw, the mention of the Torah as a unified and recognized composition is foreign to Moses's Blessing, and its appearance in verses 2 and 4 is secondary (ibid., Chap. 4, paragraph 3).

apparently, short scrolls that contained various ritual instructions regarding the work of bringing sacrifices, laws, and ceremonies of purity and impurity, etc. Remnants of these compositions are embedded in the priestly laws in the books of Leviticus and Numbers.[8]

This picture is also consistent with the history of literature as it is reflected in archaeological findings and the development of literacy in Israel. The priestly teachings "Torot", are short, technical compositions that were composed and preserved in the elite educated circles of the priesthood. Meaning, the existence of this type of literature is not dependent on the existence of a broad circle of readers or widespread literacy. Just the reverse is true, it was the share of experts and those with knowledge of the cult who transmitted their knowledge to a limited circle. Therefore, these short cultic compositions, could exist and develop as the early as beginning of of the monarchy and royal cult.[9]

In addition to the teachings תורות, Levi's blessing also refers to "ordinances"משפטים (Deut 33:10): "Teach Jacob your ordinances". It is possible that here the blessing is referring to the dealings of priests in secular matters, such as sitting in judgement, and settling conflicts between people. References to the role of priests as judges are preserved in several sources from the end of the monarchy and onwards, such as the regulations regarding the legal system in Deuteronomy (Deut. 17: 9,12; 32:5; Ezekiel 44: 33-34). In this case as well, it seems that this is an expertise that was limited to a closed circle of educated people.[10]

Let us compare the picture that arises from Levi's blessing to the rest of the traditions of the giving of the law by the water. Psalm 81 establishes that the commandments that Israel were tested on were obeying God and serving Him alone (Psalms 81:9-10):

> Hear, O my people, while I admonish you;
> O Israel, if you would but listen to me!
> There shall be no strange god among you;
> you shall not bow down to a foreign god.

---

[8] Begrich (1935).

[9] See Chap. 1 and the literature there.

[10] It is fitting that the instruction of law in Levi's blessing was made dependent on the giving of the Urim and Thummim (Deut. 33:8). Apparently, the oracle also served as a tool for the judgement of God's law on both secular and ritual issues. See Van Dam (1997, 169–176). Another similar position on the history of the law in the Hebrew Bible and the ancient Near East can be seen in Westbrook (1985, specifically pp. 257–258). He suggests that legal compositions were first composed orally, then written down, and finally integrated into a narrative-theological context in which God is the legislator.

This is also the case in the description of the Israelite's rebellion, expressed by disregarding God's word (verses 12-14):

> "But my people did not listen to my voice;
> Israel would not submit to me.
> So I gave them over to their stubborn hearts,
> to follow their own counsels.
> O that my people would listen to me,
> that Israel would walk in my ways!

As you may remember, this description is similar in its spirit and content to texts at the beginning of the Ten Commandments (Exodus 20: 2-5), which demand exclusive worship of God.[11]

Additionally, we have found echoes of the tradition of the making of the covenant at the water in the prophecies of Jeremiah. As you may remember, the speech in Jeremiah 7: 21-24 relays how Israel broke the covenant that was made with God right when they left Egypt. This covenant did not include ritual instruction, and did not even demand sacrificial worship, but rather loyalty to God, and obeying His words.[12] The breaking of the covenant is described similarly to the way it is described in Psalms 81 (Jeremiah 7: 24):

> "Yet they did not obey or incline their ear, but, in the stubbornness of their evil will, they walked in their own counsels and looked backward rather than forward."

Both this description and its sibling in Psalms 81 are, in the end, very short and indefinite. It is hard to extract very many details regarding the written form and content of the tradition the poet in Psalms and the prophet are referring to. This is also true in the case of the additional narrative of the tradition of the law near the water in the story of Marah (Exodus 15:22-26). It too uses non-specific language, "there the LORD

---

[11] See above, Chap. 5, section "Habakuk 3".

[12] As I have hinted throughout the discussion, the rejection of sacrificial worship is characteristic of the prophetic heritage in the north. It first appears in the prophecies of Amos (5:25) and Hosea (3;4) and then in the prophecies of Jeremiah, the prophet from Anatot in Benjamin (Jeremiah 7:21). As mentioned, in the book of the covenant꞉ the northern author does not reject the rites but removes from them all decorative elements or splendor. (above paragraph 1).

made for them a statute and an ordinance" without stipulating the details of the commandments and laws in the covenant between God and His people.

However, Jeremiah's additional prophecies could serve as a connecting thread between the tradition of the spring and the content of the covenant that was made there. In another prophecy he establishes that the covenant that was made when Israel left Egypt obligated the release of the Israelite slave after seven years of servitude (Jeremiah 34:13-14):

> "Thus says the LORD, the God of Israel: I myself made a covenant with your ancestors when I brought them out of the land of Egypt, out of the house of slavery, saying, "Every seventh year each of you must set free any Hebrews who have been sold to you and have served you six years; you must set them free from your service."

Meaning, according to Jeremiah, the laws that were given at the Exodus from Egypt included the obligation to release the Israelite slave during the seventh year.

So, the shards of the tradition of the water, such as the story of the waters of Marah, Psalms 81, and Jeremiah 7, indicate that the covenant in this tradition did not obligate sacrificial service, but rather demanded exclusivity to God and loyalty to His words as well as the demand to release the Israelite slave every seventh year.

C

After the story of the revelation at Sinai in chapters 19-20, Exodus 21 begins with a collection of laws under the following heading: "These are the ordinances that you shall set before them" (Exodus 21:1). And what is the first law in that collection? (21: 2):

> "When you buy a male Hebrew slave, he shall serve six years, but in the seventh he shall go out a free person, without debt."

The secondary clauses of this law continue in verses 3-6. The text then proceeds with a series of laws in casuistic structures; that is to say, laws that deal with an individual situation and open with the words, "(and) when", each representing distinctive scenarios. This sequence is not organized, and the casuistic structure appears intermittently until the law of one who seduces a virgin in 22:15-16.[13]

The parallels between the collection of laws in Exodus 21-22:16 and collections of laws in the ancient Near-East, specifically the Hammurabi Code, is well known.[14] It is this similarity between the collection and the structure of the content and style of other collections from the region that proves its relative earliness. The collection in Exodus reflects the compositions and law that were common before the rise of the primary legislative schools in the Hebrew Bible such as the Deuteronomistic school and its priestly sibling. I believe that we might assume the existence of some sort of casuistic legal structure before the eighth century BCE. It is during this period that the tradition of the spring, or at the very least Levi's blessing and Psalm 81, appear. The content of the covenant—essentially the law—that is reflected in the shards of this tradition included the obligation to remain loyal and exclusive to God, and to reject idol worship. The later and more hazy echoes of the tradition in Jeremiah 7 and the story of the waters of Marah also reflect this content. And so, it seems that there is a certain amount of ideological and substantial closeness between the adaptation of the casuistic collection at the hands of the northern legislator during the eighth century BCE and the traces of the tradition of the covenant on the water. In any case, it follows that the casuistic law and some sort of version of the Ten Commandments existed at an early stage

---

[13] For a description of the foundations of this structure and its distinction from the apodictic structure, see Alt, Israelite Law.

[14] Though my late teacher Moshe Greenberg maintained that Hebrew Biblical law was distinct from its external parallels in their moral underpinnings (Greenberg 1961), it has been noted recently, that the rejection of punishment by renumeration and ransoming of the soul are already found in a document from Mari from eighteenth century BCE, a source more or less from the same time as the Code of Hammurabi; see Bloch and Wasserman (2021). An attempt to analyze all the parallels systematically and inclusively to the Code of Hammurabi in extensive detail was made by Wright (2009). He concluded that the parallels are the result of a direct connection between the Hebrew and Akkadian sources and at the foundation of the book of the covenant (Exodus 20-24) is a direct adaptation of the Code of Hammurabi. However, as I will discuss in detail later, his analysis is complicated and is too sophisticated for its own good. Moreover, I reject the historical background that he establishes for the creation of the book of the covenant (according to him, in Jerusalem between the end of the eighth century and the beginning of the seventh century, BCE. See, Wright, ibid., 343–344).

alongside the early poetic tradition of the spring which was adapted into its current form by the northern author.[15]

Support for the cohesion and early date of the casuistic collection can be found in its numerical structure. This has been discussed by my predecessors.[16] The collection starts with a sequence of ten scenarios presented by the word, "when".[17] Nine of the first passages open in this way, while the tenth, which closes the sequence, uses the word "when" in the middle of the scenario it presents. (Exodus 20:14). The first two cases deal with slavery while the rest of them deal with bodily injury and death, from human injury to the injury of oxen. One group of laws can be set apart from this whole. It delineates seven types of bodily harm, some of which also lead to property damage. Each one of these seven cases begin with "when".[18] In comparison, the casuistic code also contains another sequence of seven scenarios that open with the word "when". Their subject are financial damages and not bodily harm.[19]

[15] The similarity of this document to the structures of more ancient works fits our ideas about the history of the law and the expansion of literacy in Israel (see paragraph 2 of this chapter above). It is natural that this type of work, which continues the pre-Biblical scribal tradition would develop among a limited circle of educated people and experts, who preserved knowledge and scribal methodologies, without the need for a broad community of readers. The distribution of the book of laws to wider circles could be done by memorization, which is supported by the numerical framework of the collection, making it easier to memorize (see below).

[16] See, Propp, **Exodus**, vol. II, 305, following August Dillmann and Benno Jacob.

[17] This is how it is divided: (1) Exodus 21:2-6 (Israelite slave) (2) 21:7-11 (Israelite female slave); (3) 21:12-17 (capital cases); (4) 21:18-19 (one who assaults a man); (5) 21: 20-21 (one who assaults a male or female slave); 6) 21:22-25 (one who hits a pregnant woman. An eye for an eye); (7) 21: 26-27 (one who disfigures a male or female slave); (8) 21:28-32 (a bull that gores); (9) 21: 33-34 (damages caused by a pit); (10) 21: 35-36 (a goring bull, one who kills a bull).

[18] (1) Exodus 21:18-19 (one who assaults a man); (2) 21: 20-21 (one who assaults a male or female slave); (3) 21:22-25 (one who hits a pregnant woman. An eye for an eye); (4) 21: 26-27 (one who disfigures a male or female slave); (5) 21:28-32 (a bull that gores); (6) 21: 33-34 (damages caused by a pit); (7) 21: 35-36 (a goring bull, one who kills a bull).

[19] (1) Exodus 21: 37-22:3 (animal theft) (2) 22:4 (*mav'eh*) (3) 22:5 (burning); (4) 22:1-8 (stealing a surety); (5) 22:9-12 (death of theft of an animal used as a deposit); (6) 22-13-14 (borrowing); (7) 22:15-16 (seducing a virgin).

Numerical structures were an important organizing principle in casuistic law.[20] It is possible that structuring the laws in this way was done to help people learn the collection by heart. This assertion fits nicely with the idea that the origin of these law is prior to the expansion of literacy during the eighth century BCE.[21]

D

I believe that it was the northern author who added the passages with apodictic wording to the casuistic legislation. These additions enclose the casuistic collection on both sides.

At the beginning of the of the reworked collection is the law of the altar which also contains the prohibition against making gods of silver and gold (Exodus 20: 19-23). This law is appropriate in light of the northern author's other arguments as we discussed above. The prohibition against idol worship is part of the rejection and denunciation of the worship of the calves, also reflected in the foundational layer of the story of the Golden Calf (Exodus 32), which was also composed by the northern writer. This is also a reflection of the author's prophetic heritage, as is implied by the similarities of his ideas to Hosea's prophecies in that they reject the idols and the calf.[22] Likewise, as we noted, the ritual regulations of the law of the altar express the desire for simpler rituals than the glorious practices common during this era. The polemical tone against the beliefs of the author's generation can also be found in the following declaration (Exodus 20:21):

---

[20] This explanation is preferable in its simplicity to the complications and complexities suggested by Wright (2009), who ascribes these things to the affinity of the collection with the Code of Hammurabi. See also bellow regarding the adaptation of the casuistic collection within the apodictic layer in the book of the covenant. For a critical evaluation of the various considerations in the analysis of the creation of the book of the covenant, including Wright's theory, see, recently Markel (2019).

[21] This was suggested to me by Propp, ibid.

[22] Though there is a distinct similarity between these texts and the later unit in Deut. 4, I tend to agree with Tigay (2004), and Feder (2013), that the texts in Exodus are earlier than the Deuteronomistic tradition, and there is reason to assume that it was influenced by Exodus and not the other way around.

"In every place where I cause my name to be remembered[23] I will come to you and bless you."

The prophecies of Amos and Hosea imply that their generation expressed their religious devotion and loyalty by streaming to pilgrimage sites related to ancient historical traditions such as Beit El, Gilgal, and Be'er Sheva (Hosea 10:5, 13:2; Amos 3:14, 4:4, 5:5, 7: 13). In contrast, the northern author maintains that it is legitimate and even desired to serve God anywhere, with God's blessing, and without the need for an honored tradition.

As is well known, the law of the altar (Exodus 20:23) is related in its language and content to the description of the revelation at Mt. Sinai which was authored by the northern author (Exodus 19:3-6). This can be seen in, among other things, the shared phrase, "you have seen", which opens both passages, as well as the egalitarian and humble worldview of ritual which is distinct from the established splendid ritual service.[24]

In addition to placing the altar law at the beginning of the casuistic collection, the northern author expanded the collection on the other side with a series of apodictic commandments. It is evident from the content of the laws that they were intended to address the social evils of the generation and the environment that the author found himself in. The laws prohibit any exploitation of the weak or oppressed such as strangers, widows, or orphans (Exodus 22:20-23). They limit the rights of debt holders to damage collateral (22: 24-26), a reality described by Amos: (2:8): "they lay themselves down beside every altar / on garments taken in pledge".

The northern author demands righteous justice and warns against taking bribery (Exodus 33:6-8), in keeping with Amos's admonition against

---

[23] Though I am well aware of the questions regarding the original version of this word, whether it is "I cause my name to be remembered", or "you cause my name to be remembered", I have decided not to discuss it here since it does not matter much to our discussion. For a discussion of the issues and the preference for the reconstruction "you cause" see Tigay (2004, 203–224); Chavel (2015, 175–170). As the latter has shown the internal dynamics of the law show that it is humanity—and not God—that sanctifies the ritual site.

[24] See, Propp, **Exodus**, vol. II, 182, as well as Chavel (2015, 179–185). However, we need to qualify some of the claims about this issue, such as the claims that the description of the establishment of the altar with the verb *'śh* (Exodus 20:20) expresses the simplicity of the rites that the law demands (Chavel, ibid., 183); compare this to the opening of the dedication of the Mesha Stele (line 3): "And I made this altar, for Chemosh" (Ahituv, **Inscriptions**, 380-282, and his comments on the site. Regarding the disestablished and egalitarian rites in the law of the altar and the worldview of the northern author see above, paragraph 1.

perverting justice of the poor (Amos 5:12). The prophet disparages and criticizes those who keep shabbat and the new month but look forward to exploitation and deceit (Amos 8:4-6). Likewise, the northern author sets down the most explicitly socially concerned wording of the shabbat in all the legislative collections in the Torah (Exodus 23:12)!

The closing of the apodictic collection comes at Exodus 23:13:

> "Be attentive to all that I have said to you. Do not invoke the names of other gods; do not let them be heard on your lips."

The language of the text echoes what was said in Exodus 20:20:

> "In every place where I cause my name to be remembered I will come to you and bless you."

The similarities between the two texts create a sort of closing door (*inclusio*). The tonal resemblance between the opening of the collection and its ending unites the adaptation and expansion of the original casuistic collection.[25]

The northern author was not satisfied with adapting the casuistic collection alone. He also embedded the adapted collection into the narrative of his creation. This narrative also expresses his revolutionary worldview. As you may remember, in the introduction to the collection he describes Israel as a kingdom of priests (Exodus 19:6):

> "But you shall be for me a priestly kingdom and a holy nation."

If this is so, then there is no need for an established religious institution. The whole nation is holy and has the right to serve in the holiest place. This idea is also implied in the prohibition against eating carrion, explained with the statement: "You shall be people consecrated to me" (Exodus 22:30). The application of this prohibition to the whole nation expresses an expansion of the circle of those who serve in the holiest places, and stands in direct opposition to the priestly worldview, which prohibits

---

[25] See Driver (1911), ad loc, as well as the introduction on pages 202–203. Toeg (1977, 114). It is possible that it is in this context that the northern background of the end of the eighth century also shows up in the works of our author: compare this to Hosea 2:18-19: " For I will remove the names of the Baals from her mouth, and they shall be mentioned by name no more."

the eating of carrion and carcasses to priests alone (Lev. 22:8; Ezekiel 44:31).[26]

An implementation of our author's position can be seen in the description of the covenant ceremony that ends the giving of the law at Sinai. It is the youth of the children of Israel who are set to work bringing sacrifices (Exodus 24:3-8):[27]

Moses went and told the people all the words of the LORD and all the ordinances, and all the people answered with one voice and said, "All the words that the LORD has spoken we will do." **4** And Moses wrote down all the words of the LORD. He rose early in the morning, built an altar at the foot of the mountain, and set up twelve pillars, corresponding to the twelve tribes of Israel. **5** He sent young men of the Israelites, who offered burnt offerings and sacrificed oxen as offerings of well-being to the LORD. **6** Moses took half of the blood and put it in basins, and half of the blood he dashed against the altar. **7** Then he took the book of the covenant and read it in the hearing of the people, and they said, "All that the LORD has spoken we will do, and we will be obedient." **8** Moses took the blood and dashed it on the people, and said, "Here is the blood of the covenant that the LORD has made with you in accordance with all these words."

In summary, it seems that the northern author and Amos the Prophet dealt with similar challenges. However, their responses to the moral injustices and the atrophied and corrupt ritual around them varied. Amos completely rejected the value of sacrifices, while the legislator sought to moderate and soften ritual sacrifice; Amos admonished and threatened his

---

[26] On the expansion of the limits of holiness as well as the circle of those serving in the holiest place see above paragraph 1, as well as Chavel's discussion (2015, 185–197). Chavel even demonstrates how pieces of the northern author's framework in Exodus 19, 20, and 24 can be consolidated into one unified and sequential subject/narrative passage.

[27] On the connection between the pieces of the framework by the northern author in Exodus 19,2, and 24 see Chavel, ibid. He demonstrates how these texts are unified into one continuous unit. As with many other issues, Deuteronomy follows in the footsteps of the northern author. See Deut. 14:21.

generation because of their corrupt ways, while the legislator responded with legislation and ritual and moral instruction.[28]

On the other hand, there is one aspect in which the northern author was more extreme than Amos. The law in Exodus 22:27 forbids cursing God or humans of high status:[29]

"You shall not revile God or curse a leader of your people".

We are mainly interested in the second clause of the verse, which forbids cursing "a leader" נשיא. Researchers have contended that this phrasing is a product of the social reality preceding the monarchy and is an expression of a tribal society and its leadership. Even though the northern author was active more than 200 years after the establishment of the monarchy in Israel, he specifically used ancient terminology from a reality that preceded that institution. This could be a literary device. Our author attributed his own words to Moses, during the wanderings in the desert. He needed to dress those words in suitable glory in order to make them believable. However, another reference to the monarchy in one of the legal collections in the Torah, those of the law of the king in Deut. 18: 14-20 proves that mentioning the monarchy is possible even for someone who worked hard to hide the true origin of their words.[30] Even more so, because the laws were intended for the future, when Israel was settled in their land, there is no real reason to avoid mentioning a king or the monarchy as part of the future political and social reality. Just the reverse is true. It is necessary given the purpose of the law.

In ignoring the monarchy and using the term נשיא "leader" which is characteristic of pre-monarchical egalitarian society, the author expresses a principled opposition to the institution of the monarchy. A similar tone is

---

[28] As is the way of the Hebrew Biblical legislator, these too were accompanied by warnings, threats, and persuasions, such Exodus 20:4,6; 22:23. However, these are mostly just anecdotes in what is essentially an overarching legal system for the nation, the likes of which cannot be found in the admonitions of the prophets mentioned above.

[29] There is reason to doubt the originality of this version. It is possible that the term "leader" took the place of the reading "king" that preceded it (compare to I Kings 21'13; Isaiah 8:21, as well as Rofé 1988). Whatever the original version of the text is, in any case there is broad circumstantial evidence for the northern author's criticism of the monarchy.

[30] Regarding the character of the Deuteronomy as pseudepigrapha and the limitations that this forced upon its composers see, among others, Smith (1971); Hoffman (1982); Weinfeld (1992, 183–184).

evident in Hosea's prophecies (Hosea 13:10-11) and the works of the "historian from Ephraim", a northern historian whose work are embedded in the Books of Joshua, Judges, and Samuel. Both, the northern author, and the historian, were active during the last days of the kingdom of Israel and expressed their bitter disappointment in the institution of the monarchy.[31] The northern author's Torah compositions are another echo of the argument regarding the status of the monarchy during its last days in Samaria.[32]

E

So, the tradition of the covenant at the water was familiar with the casuistic collection of laws embedded in Exodus 20-22. This collection was an ancient document that was composed before the eighth century BCE as well as the expansion of literacy in Israel.[33] It was assembled by a northern

[31] Regarding this work and its connection to the prophecies of Hosea see Rofé (1991).

[32] This is emphasized in Chavel (2015). I recently discussed the northern opposition to the monarchy in two places: See, Knohl (2019, 27–44), as well as Knohl (2023, 181–182). Another, slightly different position regarding the development of the version of the text in Exodus 22:27 is held by Rofé (1988), followed by Wright (2009, 297–298). They believe that "Nasi, Chieftain" is a late edition inspired by the ongoing disagreement regarding the status of the monarch (which they also believe originates in the last generations of the kingdom of Israel). However, this is an edit and not an original text and it is difficult to distinguish between later adaptations of the text and original versions that reflect earlier stages in the disagreement, such as the reminiscences of the kingdom of God and those who were saved in Obadiah 1:21 (Those who have been saved shall go up to Mount Zion/ to rule Mount Esau,/ and the kingdom shall be the LORD's).

[33] An additional argument, and the last one in our discussion, for concluding that the northern author's work can be found in the "lowest level" of Deuteronomy: As is well known, the collection of laws in Deuteronomy is an adaptation of the book of the covenant. It is adapted in such a way that is very similar to the assumed composition of the northern author. Attributing Deut. 12-26 to the second half of the seventh century BCE following the lead of W.M.L. deWette, indicates that the works of the northern author preceded this period by as much as a generation or two, as expected by its acceptance as authoritative among the Jerusalemite scribes. This places us at the earliest in the last decade of the eighth century BCE. The composition's similarities to the northern prophets and northern polemics against the worship of the calves shows that the date of the composition needs to be pushed back at least another generation when Samaria stood. Regarding the adaptation of the book of the covenant in the collection of laws in Deuteronomy see Chavel (2015, 202–207) and before him Otto (1996); Levinson (1997).

A similar position to the one expressed here was recently expressed by Jiang (2022). He also believes that the casuistic laws existed first, and the direct Divine commandments were

author who was active in the latter half of the eighth century BCE in the kingdom of Israel. This northern author adapted the ancient casuistic law in various ways, mainly by merging it with apodictic laws. His legislation is based on impressively expressed moral principles.

The northern author's moral legislation goes hand in hand with his ritual legislation and worldview. He emphasized the demand for folk rites and rejected the ostentatious monarchy-sponsored worship of the idols in the north. According to this author-legislator, the whole nation is a "kingdom of priests and holy nation" and therefore also have the right to serve in the holiest of places, and, in keeping with that, the obligations of purity and morality fall upon them just as it does the members of the priesthood. In this way the anonymous northern author tried to deal with and respond to the disorder and defects of the society he was active in. His methodology is distinct from the position of the prophets of his time, such as Amos and Hosea. He took a more moderate positive line than the zealous prophets and sought to rebuild the rites and guide the nation to moral behavior. At the same time, similarly to Hosea and other northern composers, he rejected the monarchy, and gave preference to the kingdom of God and tribal leadership as described in the times of the Judges.

BIBLIOGRAPHY

J. Begrich, 1935, "Die priestliche Torah", in P. Volz et al. (eds.), *Werden und Wesen des Alten Testaments* (BZAW 66), Berlin, 63–88.

J. Blenkinsopp, 1999, "Deuteronomic Contribution to the Narrative in Genesis — Numbers: A Test Case", in: L.S. Schearing and S. L. McKenzie (eds.), *Those Elusive Deuteronomists: The Phenomenon of 'Pandeuteronomism'* (JSOTSup. 268), Sheffield, 84–115.

Y. Bloch and N. Wasserman, 2021, "Blood Guilt and Monetary Compensation in Biblical Laws and Mari Letters", *Beit Mikra* 66, 7–32 [in Hebrew].

S. Chavel, 2015, "A Kingdom of Priests and its Earthen Altars in Exodus 19-24", *VT* 65, 169–222.

S.R. Driver, 1911, *Exodus* (CB), Cambridge.

added during a secondary edition. In addition, he also believes that the collection that is known as "the book of the covenant" was consolidated as a response to admonitions from the prophets of that generation. However, he establishes the location of its creation as Judah at the end of the eighth century BCE and identifies the influence of the admonitions of Isaiah son of Amoz and Micha from Morasha in the collection. However, I believe that the northern background of the author of the book of the covenant is evident in additional places as I discussed in other parts of the discussion.

Y. Feder, 2013, "The Aniconic Tradition, Deuteronomy 4 and the Politics of Israelite Identity", *JBL* 132, 251–274.

I. Finkelstein, 2013, *The Forgotten Kingdom: The Archaeology and History of Northern Israel*, Atlanta GA.

M. Greenberg, 1961, "Some Postulates of Biblical Criminal Law", in: M. Haran (ed.), *Yehezkel Kaufmann Jubilee Volume*, Jerusalem, 5–28.

Y. Hoffman, 1982, "Exigencies of Genre in Deuteronomy", *Shnaton* 5–6, 41–54 [in Hebrew].

S. Jiang, 2022, "How Prophecy Critiquing Socio-Economic Injustice Transformed into Law: The Cases of the Covenant Code and Early Prophetic Texts", *ZAW* 134, 441–457.

I. Knohl, 2019, *The Messiah Controversy: Who Are the Jews Waiting For?*, Tel Aviv [in Hebrew].

I. Knohl, 2023, (Recension:[S. Ahituv, *Hosea* (Mikra Leyisrael), Tel Aviv 2022]), *Beit Mikra* 68, 177–182.

B.M. Levinson, 1997, *Deuteronomy and the Hermeneutics of Legal Innovation*, Oxford.

D. Markel, 2019, "The Redactional Theologization of the Book of the Covenant: A Study in Criteriology", *BN* 181, 47–61.

S. Olyan, 1996, "Why an Altar of Unfinished Stones? Some Thoughts on Ex 20, 25 and Dtn 27, 5-6", *ZAW* 108, 161–171.

Eckart Otto, 1996, "The Pre-exilic Deuteronomy as a Revision of the Covenant Code", in: idem, *Kontinuum und Proprium. Studien zur Sozial- und Rechtsgeschichte des Alten Orients und des Alten Testaments, Orientalia Biblica et Christiana*, Wiesbaden, 112–122.

A. Rofé, 1988, "Qumranic Paraphrases, the Greek Deuteronomy and the Late History of the Biblical נשיא", *Textus* 14, 163–174.

A. Rofé, 1991, "Ephraimite versus Deuteronomistic history", in: D. Garrone and F. Israel (eds.), *Storia e tradizioni di Israele; scritti in onore di J. Alberto Soggin*, Brecia, 221–235.

Morton Smith, 1971, "Pseudoepigraphy in the Israelite Tradition" (1971), repr. in S.J.D. Cohen (ed.), *Studies in the Cult of Yahwe*, I-II, Leiden 1995–1996, I, 55–72.

J.H. Tigay, 2004, "The Presence of God and the Coherence of Exodus 20:22-26", in: C. Cohen et al. (eds.), *Sefer Moshe: The Moshe Weinfeld Jubilee Volume*, Winona Lake IN, 195–211.

A. Toeg, 1977, *Lawgiving at Sinai*, Jerusalem [in Hebrew].

C. Van Dam, 1997, *The Urim and Thummim: A Means of Revelation in Ancient Israel*, Winona Lake IN.

J. Van Seters, 1999, "Is There Evidence of a Dtr Redaction in the Sinai Pericope (Exodus 19-24, 32-34)?", in: L.S. Schearing and S. L. McKenzie (eds.),Those

84   I. KNOHL

Elusive Deuteronomists: The Phenomenon of 'Pandeuteronomism' (JSOTSup. 268), Sheffield, 160–170.

M. Weinfeld, 1992, *From Joshua to Josiah: Turning Points in the History of Israel from the Conquest of the Land Until the Fall of Judah*, Jerusalem [in Hebrew].

R. Westbrook, 1985, "Biblical and Cuneiform Law Codes", *RB* 92, 247–264.

D.P. Wright, 2009, *Inventing God's Law: How the Covenant Code of the Bible Used and Revised the Laws of Hammurabi*, New York-Oxford.

CHAPTER 10

An Egalitarian Revelation by the Water, a Private Revelation at the Mountain

A

Now that we have the general outline of the tradition of northern legislation, we must delve into some of the perceivable changes that occurred during the transition from the poetic tradition of the revelation by the water to the narrative tradition of the covenant at Sinai.

One prominent aspect of the poetic tradition is the egalitarian nature of the revelation contained in it. Its poetic echoes describe direct communication between God and His people. This is the case in Psalms 81: 9-11: God addresses the whole nation (Verse 9: Hear, O my people, while I admonish you;/ O Israel, if you would but listen to me!), and His demand for exclusivity is addressed to all those who share in the covenant (verses 10-11). The same can be said for the narrative and prophetic echoes of the tradition of the spring revelation. They too seem to indicate a group revelation without a mediator. The end of the story of the waters of Marah is addressed to the whole nation (Exodus 15:25-26: There the LORD made for them a statute and an ordinance, and there he put them to the test. He said, "If you will listen carefully to the voice of the LORD your God...").[1] So too, in the mention of the covenant in Jeremiah's speech in Jeremiah 7:23: (Obey my voice, and I will be your God, and you shall be my people).

---

[1] Though Moses is mentioned in the story of the waters of Marah, his role is limited to sweetening the water and he has no role in making the covenant or giving the laws.

I. Knohl, *Biblical Sinai traditions*, https://doi.org/10.1007/978-3-031-77983-1_10

The remnants of the tradition of the spring do not attribute the role of legislator to Moses.

Another characteristic aspect of this tradition is the serene character of revelation. It is not frightening or accompanied by storms or volcanic phenomena such as those that are described in the revelation at Sinai-Horeb (Exodus 19:12-19; 20, 14; Deut. 5: 4, 19-23). Though the arrival of God and His journey to the location of the revelation is accompanied by earthquakes and volcanic eruptions, these are disparate from the descriptions of the revelation and the covenant themselves.[2] The revelation by the water was serene. It did not frighten the assembly making the covenant.

The narrative tradition of the revelation at Sinai is distinct from its poetic fellow in the two aspects that I mentioned above. The characteristics of the revelation that is described in Exodus 19 (and its parallel in Deut. 5) are not populist or folk-centered in the same way as they are in the poetic descriptions. Though indeed the whole nation stands at the foot of the mountain and hears the commandments from God, in a similar manner to the direct communication in the poems, Moses's role as the mediator in communicating with God, the giving of the laws, and the ability of the nation to withstand the entire event, is emphasized. Moses's prominence is intertwined with the frightening description of the verbal revelation by the mountain. The nation is afraid of their proximity to the Divine, the agitation of nature and the rest of the fearful elements related to the giving of the laws (Exodus 19: 19, 20: 15).

There is reason to contend that the northern narrator was familiar with some sort of version of the ancient poetic tradition. He was active in prophetic circles close to the northern temples in which the oral poetry was transmitted.[3] It seems right to assume that he combined elements of the poetic tradition that were originally separate. He duplicated the description of the direct revelation from the setting of the spring to a mountainous-volcanic setting. He combined the poetic descriptions of the volcanic phenomena and the earthquakes during God's journey from His abode in

---

[2] Regarding the volcanic activity that accompanies God's arrival from Sinai in Moses's Blessings, the Song of Deborah, Habakkuk 3, and Psalm 68, see above, Chaps. 2, 3, and 4, as well as the studies of Amzallag (2014), Dunn (2014). Also worthy of mentioning are the more general studies by Loewenstamm (1964), and Weinfeld (1978).

[3] The ritual background of Psalm 81 is clear from its opening (verses 2-5). Regarding the ritual background of Moses's Blessings, see Cassuto, Deuteronomy 33. Seeligmann (1964, 201–204) also believed that Moses's Blessings had a ceremonial-ritual background but suggested a different context and character than Cassuto.

Sinai and God's revelation and the giving of laws to His people. These processes nullified the primary characteristics of the revelation in the poetic tradition: from a serene revelation, lawgiving, and a covenant by the water, to an impressive and scary revelation and covenant at the mountain. This also reveals the secondary nature of the narrative tradition and its dependence on the poetic tradition: the narrative tradition uproots the motif of a volcanic revelation from its natural and original context in the volcanic region Edom-Midian and placed it in the region close to Egypt in the Sinai Peninsula which is not volcanic at all. This discrepancy shows how the narrative tradition distanced itself from the original descriptions of the volcanic revelation which suited the location's geographic reality.[4]

As mentioned, the nation's fear is emphasized in the description by the northern author (Exodus 19:19; 20:15). The horrifying spectacle of voices/sounds, lightning, the smoking mountain, and the Divine voice was beyond their capabilities. That is why they asked for a mediator to distance them from the inherent danger of being in proximity to that which is holy (Exodus 20: 15):

"..and said to Moses, "You speak to us, and we will listen, but do not let God speak to us, lest we die."

And though Moses agrees to their request he implores them (verse 16):

"Moses said to the people, "Do not be afraid, for God has come only to test you and to put the fear of him upon you so that you do not sin."

According to the northern author the purpose of the revelation was to test Israel and teach them to fear their God.[5] However, Moses's entreaty did not put the nation's fears to rest. They distanced themselves from the

---

[4] We should note Loewenstamm (1964, 510), and his discussion regarding the verb חר״ד, *hrd*, "feared". This verb is foreign to descriptions of earthquakes during the revelation in the poetry found the prophetic literature and psalms. In general, Loewenstamm has clearly and methodologically demonstrated how the poetic tradition regarding the revelation at Sinai is separate from the narrative tradition in Exodus and also earlier than it.

[5] It's possible that the phrase "test you" means withstanding a test (compare to Deut.8:2; it is possible that this is an additional paraphrase of the tradition of the spring. Compare to Exodus 15:25: "There the LORD made for them a statute and an ordinance, and there he put them to the test."); it is also possible that the meaning of the phrase here is: to learn and gain experience, and in that context- recognize the experience of Divine revelation. (This is Greenberg's opinion, 1960; compare to Deut. 8:16; I Samuel 17:39).

mountain and from then onwards the laws were transmitted to Moses, who ascended to God, alone (verses 17-18). Meaning, it was the nation's fear that led to their distance from the holy and the need for the prophet's mediation.

B

What motivated the northern author to change the nature of the revelation and the giving of the laws in the way that he did? I believe that the explanation for this lies in the revolutionary subversive nature of the collection of laws which he attributed to Moses at Sinai (that is to say, the reworked and expanded book of the covenant). This can be seen in the unique character of the collection. On the one hand, its origins are mysterious, but on the other, this very mystery grants the laws authority. As mentioned, in Exodus 20: 17-18 Moses is established as the mediator between the nation and God. From then on, the laws would be given to him alone:

> "Then the people stood at a distance, while Moses drew near to the thick darkness where God was. The LORD said to Moses…"

The collection of laws ends with Moses's return to the nation and the transmission of the laws that were given during the time he was alone in the Divine darkness (Exodus 24:3):

> "Moses went and told the people all the words of the LORD and all the ordinances…"

The origin of the northern narrator's collection of laws is wrapped in mystery. Where did it come from? God gave it to Moses directly without witnesses: of the event, or the content of the laws. The law is only elucidated to the people after Moses returns.

Camouflaging the origins of a narrative creation while attributing it to a famous historical figure is a well-known tactic used by revolutionary and subversive authors who wish to give their compositions validity and authority. This can be seen in the pseudo-epigraphy of the Apocrypha, and hints to this method in Hebrew Biblical literature can be found as early as the end of the monarchy.[6]

This sort of pseud-epigraphy is necessary, as mentioned, due to the revolutionary and subversive nature of the northern author's legislation. We have discussed the way in which he dismissed widespread ritual traditions in the northern kingdom and his attempt to respond to the criticisms of prophets such as Amos and Hosea against the nation's religious behavior. We also saw the author's criticism of the moral behavior of the Israelite elite and the institution of the monarchy.[7] The very fact that he opened his collection of laws with ritual legislation that rejects the worship of the royal calves as well as the grand temples of the north (Exodus 20: 18-22), is a declaration of war against the official religion of the kingdom in which he lived and wrote. It is doubtful whether his words would be received or tolerated quietly unless he attributed the laws to Moses and the revelation at Sinai.

Another way in which he granted authority to his legislation is reflected in the ceremony of the covenant that is at the end of the northern collection of laws (Exodus 24 and on). Moses transmits the laws that he heard from God to the nation, and after they declare that they accept them, Moses writes the covenant into a book. Afterwards monuments are erected, sacrifices are made, and there is a feast.[8] This description provides the collection of laws with authority in several ways. First, it gives validity to the covenant. This can be seen, for instance, in the fact that the covenant is read out loud and subsequently accepted by the nation (Exodus 24: 7):

> "Then he took the book of the covenant and read it in the hearing of the people, and they said, "All that the LORD has spoken we will do, and we will be obedient.""

This is also the case with regards to the symbolic act of spraying the blood in verse 8:

---

[6] My intention is of course the attribution of Deuteronomy and the collection of laws in it to Moses. Regarding pseudo-epigraphy in the Hebrew composition of the Hebrew Bible and post-Biblical literature, see, Smith (1971).

[7] See the previous chapter.

[8] The ceremony is in keeping with parallel examples in ancient Near-Eastern literature. See Weinfeld, Covenant.

"Moses took the blood and dashed it on the people, and said, "Here is the blood of the covenant that the LORD has made with you in accordance with all these words.""

This description gives the northern author's collection of laws a sense of antiquity and authority. He establishes its going into effect as early as the days of the wanderings in the desert and Moses's leadership. Meaning, the covenant and its laws have been obligatory since then and up to the days of the northern author. Neglecting its existence is a sin.

The covenant and its ceremonies are held according to the ritual regulations of the northern author. Moses erects an inglorious altar and monuments (verse 4), in keeping with the rules at the beginning of the collection (Exodus 20:20-21). Those who serve in the holiest of places are "the young men of the Israelites" (Exodus 24:5), and not the closed circle of priests, congruent with the statement at the beginning of the story of revelation that Israel will be "a priestly kingdom and a holy nation" (Exodus 19:6). The covenant ceremony not only marks the coming into effect of the laws, but also presents a precedent for their existence during the desert generation. In this way the northern author's demands are not a revolution but the return to previous glory and the reinstatement of ritual as it once was.[9]

C

By setting his collection of laws in the dress of the desert wanderings and attributing them to Moses, the northern author was able to confront the various issues he was fighting against head on. It provides his composition with authority vis a vis the monarchy, the priesthood, and the elite as well as the circles of prophets that criticized them. In order to accomplish this, the northern author revolutionized Israelite historical tradition.

The figure of Moses was known in Israelite tradition during the time of the northern legislator. This can be clearly seen in the hints to a prophet

---

[9] The analogy to Deuteronomy is clear: It too is attributed to Moses and the desert era as a source of authority for a book that was "discovered" many generations later, during the reign of Josiah. However, in contrast to Deuteronomy, which sets the stage for its rediscovery in the etiology in Deut. 31, there is nothing that remains from the northern author's composition that prepares the reader for a rediscovery of the book of the covenant in the future.. A number of people have commented on the etiology in Deuteronomy 31. See, for instance, Richard Friedman (1981), and Zevit (2009).

who takes Israel out of Egypt in the prophecies of Hosea (Hosea 12:14), as well as references to Moses soon after the time of the northern prophet (II Kings 18, 4; Micah 6:3-4).[10] However, Moses rarely appears as a legislative figure outside of Hebrew Biblical literature until much later.[11] And when he is mentioned in early Hebrew Biblical literature, he is mentioned as a leader during the time of the exodus from Egypt and the wanderings in the desert.[12]

The northern author adopted the familiar figure of Moses from the well-known tradition during his time and granted that figure with the legislative characteristics reflected in the story of the revelation at Sinai and the covenant. Now, the prophet not only brings the word of God, but is a mediator in the giving of the Divine law and the covenant between the nation and its God. This turning point in the metamorphosis of the traditions regarding Moses, is, of course, an incredible revolution in the history of Israelite and Jewish culture. And so it is that the opening of the Tractate Aboth in the Mishna: "Moses Received the Torah at Sinai", has its roots in his revolutionary works.[13]

[10] It seems that the northern psalm 77 can be added to this list as well as the mention of Moses and Samuel in Jeremiah 15:1. The very fact that Moses is mentioned shows that his figure was, at the very least, a part of Israelite tradition. We can assume that his stories came into being before the time of Hosea and the rest of the sources mentioned here. This assumption might be supported by the Egyptian origin of the name Moses (see Ahituv, Moses, 496; Griffiths 1953). In addition, his connection to the Midianites and marriage to the daughter of the priest of Midian were most certainly not accepted at a later stage in the history of Hebrew Biblical literature, which proceeded to invalidate the Midianites and negated the Israelite's connection with them (see for instance Numbers 25, 31). The many faces and aspects of the figure of Moses in Hebrew Biblical composition, as well as the complicated attitude towards him are proof that the traditions about him were compiled over many generations and are not a pat creation that was formed all at once. It could even indicate the existence of a true historical kernel behind the traditions. Regarding the Moses tradition in the Hebrew Bible see a survey of the sources and the discussion in Widengren (1970), as well as Blum's updated evaluation, 2012. For previous scholarship on the subject see, Otto (2007, 21–27); Ehrlich (2012); Römer (2015).

[11] In the Torah narrative and the early prophets, the figure of Moses as a legislator is characteristic of priestly compositions and Deuteronomy and the Deuteronomistic edition of the early prophets; that is to say, this aspect of his figure is emphasized mostly during the latter days of the kingdom of Judah. Moses is not mentioned as a legislator in ancient poetry (the text in Deut. 33:4, is, as mentioned, a later insertion from the time of the return to Zion), and in prophetic literature he appears as a legislator only in Malachi 3:22.

[12] This was preserved up until later generations. See Isaiah 63:11-12.

[13] There is a huge amount of literature on the tradition of Moses in the Hebrew Bible and outside of it, and this is not the place to survey it. See footnote 301, below. For another

D

Another departure from the poetic tradition that was inserted by the northern author relates to the breaking of the covenant immediately after it was made and shortly after the giving of the laws. The poetic tradition describes a rebellion on the water related to serving other gods, while the description by the northern author applied these details to the sin of the golden calf (Exodus 33). It is possible that he borrowed details from the poetic tradition in this context as well, such as the setting of the spring in Exodus 32:20.[14] As with the other details that were borrowed for the narrative from the poetry, here two things were required to change the structure of the tradition. The most prominent of them in this context is that the northern author uprooted the location of the spring and established it close to Horeb-Sinai, not far from the border of Egypt. In the poetic tradition the spring at the waters of Meribah is close to Egypt but very far from Sinai which is in Edom-Midian.[15]

The description of the sin of the Golden Calf gives us insight into the northern author's activities. After the sin there is a second revelation on the mountain and a renewal of the covenant (Exodus 33-34). This description is clearly parallel to the series of stories regarding Elijah in I Kings 17-19.[16] The story of Elijah also involves the breaking of the covenant via

opinion regarding Moses's relationship to the law see, Nielsen, 1982. I disagree with his analysis regarding the history of Hebrew Biblical literature and am also doubtful whether the bronze snake is a northern symbol, as he contends. This symbol is primarily mentioned in a Judahite context, and archeological findings connect it to this area, see the symbol of the snake on an altar found in Be'er Sheba (Aharoni 1974). The works of DeJong (2022), and Stackert (2014), focused on later stages in the history of the traditions regarding Moses and his relationship to the law, starting from the Deuteronomy and the schola that composed it.

[14] Regarding the setting of the spring: compare this to the parallel description in Deut. 9:21, which specifically notes "the stream that runs down the mountain". Regarding the spring in the background of the story of the golden calf, see also Propp (1987, 61–63).

[15] Another expression of this upheaval is the identification of Repidim with Massah and Meribah by a later editor (Exodus 17: 1-7, esp. 2,7), see MacDonald, 2012. Regarding the later priestly version in Numbers 20:1-13, see Knohl (1995, 94–96).

[16] The similarities between Moses and Elijah have been discussed in the past, and there is a lot of literature on the subject. In keeping with this- there are a lot of various opinions on the matter. There are those who see appropriation from one place to the other and its reverse, while others identify a pattern, or a joint foundational tradition to the two stories. Given the lack of additional information, it is better to be cautious and be satisfied in pointing out the similarities between the traditions. There is enough evidence to conclude that they come from the same circles. For previous discussions see Procksch (1906, 246ff). Zakovitch (1982,

worship of the Ba'al, then a battle against the followers of the Ba'al on the Carmel (I Kings 18), and a revelation at Horeb (19).[17] The similarities between the social and ritual opinions of the northern author and the reality as reflected in the stories of Elijah are also notable: despite the fact that the prophet is not a priest, he performs sacrifices (I Kings 18). His student, Elisha, also does so. He performs sacrifices at his parents' house even though he is not a priest (19:19-21). Though Elijah does relate importance to ritual and sees it as an important expression of the covenant with God (I Kings19:1), he also expresses moral criticism of the rulers (I Kings 21:17-19; compare with II Kings 9:25-26).[18] Elijah's social reality also fits the spirit of the northern author's legislation. The sons of the prophets, those who accompanied them, and the supporters of Elijah and Elisha lived simple and communal lives. There is a similarity between the social ideas that guided them and the spirit of the social laws that the northern author added to the book of the covenant.

It seems to me that we must assume that these similarities are not accidental, and that the northern author worked in close cooperation with the followers of the prophets in which the traditions about Elijah and Elisha blossomed. Though we do not know what happened to those circles in the generations after Elisha, over the course of the eighth century BCE,[19] it seems that the traditions that they created were transmitted to the next generations to the extent that they were integrated into the Book of Kings by Judean circles at the end of the monarchy and afterwards. In any case, it seems that the northern author of the Torah worked in some sort of closeness to the creators of the traditions of the sons of the prophets who were active in the north and was influenced by them just as he was influenced by Amos's admonitions.

344–346); Jenks (1977, 93ff); Seidel (1993), Gnuse (2000). See also Roi (2012) regarding the narrative pattern of the journey, including the narratives of Moses and Elijah.

[17] In addition to the well-known similarities between the descriptions of the revelation at Horeb (see for instance Zakovitch, ibid., Seidel, ibid.), we should also note the possibility that Elijah's revelation also has a volcanic foundation, see the suggestion of Dunn (2014, 415–417).

[18] Even if we accept Rofé's opinion, (Rofé 1988b), according to which the story of the Naboth's vineyard was composed during the days of the return to Zion, the text of the story of Jehu's rebellion shows that it is an ancient tradition (this is his opinion as well, see ibid., 95–97).

[19] There is perhaps one final echo in Amos's words to Amazia the priest of Beit El (Amos 7:12-15), and they perhaps indicate some sort of shirking away from or at the very least isolation from those circles.

This fits the estimated period of time that was suggested above for the northern author's activities, in the second half of the eighth century BCE, towards the final days of the northern kingdom.[20] The stories of Elijah retain the memory of the Aramean persecution of the ninth century (I Kings 19: 17-18), but are not aware of the demand for the consolidation of the rites which only came to be during Hezekiah's reforms at the end of the eighth century BCE.[21]

The northern author's prophetic background fits the central place that he gave the figure of Moses as a legislator and a mediator between the nation and their God. This is very different from the poetic tradition regarding the covenant and its breaking, which does not relate to Moses and does not give him a role in the proceedings. This is also the case regarding the narrative and prophetic echoes of the traditions in Marah and Jeremiah: though both were aware of the figure of Moses, they do not attribute to him characteristics of a legislator or a mediator in the giving of the laws. The northern author, was, as mentioned above, the one who emphasized the role of Moses in the covenant and the giving of the laws, as well as the importance of the institution of prophecy and the status of the prophets. This is in keeping with his palpable closeness to the circles that transmitted the stories of Elijah and Elisha. In those circles the prophet was admired for their miracles, the words of the God that they transmitted as well as their ability to tell the future. This was replicated into the description of Moses as a mediating figure between God and His nation by the northern author.

The northern author drew from many sources. He possessed the poetic tradition regarding the making of the covenant and its breaking by the water, as well as the legacy of the circle of the sons of the prophets, of which, perhaps he was a member or one of their successors. He borrowed various motifs from his sources and combined them. The volcanic revelation, the law giving and the breaking of the covenant with idolatry. All these motifs and memories were combined now with the figure of the prophet as a mediator between the nation and their God, the one who renews the covenant, the admonisher, and warrior against idolatry. These

---

[20] See the previous chapter.
[21] See Rofé (1988a, 165 ff). He establishes the latest time regarding the consolidation of rites as Josiah's regulations, and in keeping with that, sees the reign of Menashe as the most fitting time for the primary creation of the Elijah stories. However, archeological evidence shows that the demand to consolidate the rites should be earlier, as can be seen by the closure of the altars at Be'er Sheba, Arad, and Lachish (Herzog 2010; Ganor and Kreimerman 2017).

issues were cast onto the ancient and authoritative figure of Moses in order to give power and validity to the legislation and revolutionary world views of the northern author.

BIBLIOGRAPHY

Y. Aharoni, 1974, "The Horned Altar of Beer-sheba", *BA* 37, 2–6.

N. Amzallag, 2014, "Some Implications of the Vulcanic Theophany of YHWH on His Primeval Identity", *Antiguo Oriente* 12, 11–38.

E. Blum, 2012, "Der historische Mose und die Frühgeschichte Israels", *HeBai* 1, 37–63.

D. DeJong, 2022, *A Prophet like Moses (Deut 18:15, 18) The Origin, History, and Influence of the Mosaic Prophetic Succession* (SJSJ 205), Leiden and Boston.

J.E. Dunn, 2014, "A God of Volcanoes: Did Yahwism Take Root in Volcanic Ashes?", *JSOT* 38, 387–424.

Carl S. Ehrlich, 2012, "'Noughty' Moses: A Decade of Moses Scholarship 2000-2010", *HeBaI* 1, 93–110.

Richard E. Friedman, 1981, "From Egypt to Egypt: Dtr1 and Dtr2", in: B. Halpern and J.D. Levenson (ed.), *Traditions in Transformation: Turning Points in Biblical Faith*, Winona Lake IN, 167–192.

S. Ganor and I. Kreimerman, 2017, "An Eighth Century B.C.E. Gate Shrine at Tel Lachish, Israel", *BASOR* 381, 211–236.

R.K. Gnuse, 2000, "Redefining the Elohist", *JBL* 119, 201–220.

M. Greenberg, 1960, "נסה in Exodus 20 20 and the Porpuse of the Sinaitic Theophany", *JBL* 79, 273–276.

J.G. Griffiths, 1953, "The Egyptian Derivation of the Name Moses", *JNES* 12, 225–231.

Z. Herzog, 2010, "Perspectives on Southern Israel's Cult Centralization: Arad and Beer-Sheba", in: R. G. Kratz and H. Spieckermann (eds.), *One God—One Cult—One Nation: Archaeological and Biblical Perspectives* (BZAW 405), Berlin, 169–199.

A. Jenks, 1977, *The Elohist and the North Israelite Traditions* (SBLMS 22), Missoula MT.

I. Knohl, 1995, *The Sanctuary of Silence: The Priestly Torah and the Holiness School*, Minneapolis.

ש"א ליונשטם, 1964, "רעדת הטבע בשעת הופעת ה'", "עז לדוד, Loewenstamm, ירושלים, 520–508.

N. MacDonald, 2012, "Anticipation of Horeb: Exodus 17 as Inner-Biblical Commentary", in: G. Khan and D. Lipton (eds.), *Studies on the Text and Versions of the Hebrew Bible in Honour of Robert Gordon*, Leiden, 7–20.

E. Nielsen, 1982, "Moses and the Law", *VT* 32, 87–98.

E. Otto, 2007, *Mose: Geschichte und Legende*, München.

O. Procksch, 1906, *Das nordhebräische Sagenbuch: Die Elohimquelle*, Leipzig.

W.H.C. Propp, 1987, *Water in the Wilderness* (HSM 68), Atlanta GA.

A. Rofé, 1988a, *The Prophetical Stories: The Narratives About the Prophets in the Hebrew Bible, Their Literary Types and History*, Jerusalem.

A. Rofé, 1988b, "The Vineyard of Naboth: The Origin and Message of the Story", *VT* 38, 89–104.

M. Roi, 2012, "The Story of Elijah's Flight (1 Kings 19): A Comparative Study on the Pattern of 'Departure Stories' in the Bible", *Shnaton* 21, 69–92 [in Hebrew].

T. Römer, 2015, *Moïse en version originale: Enquête sur le récit de la sortie d'Égypte*.

I.L. Seeligmann, 1964, "A Psalm from Pre-Regal Times", *VT* 14, 75–92.

Theodor Seidl, 1993, "Mose und Elija am Gottesberg: Überlieferungen zu Krise und Konversion der Propheten", *BZ* 37, 1–25.

Morton Smith, 1971, "Pseudoepigraphy in the Israelite Tradition" (1971), repr. in S.J.D. Cohen (ed.), *Studies in the Cult of Yahwe*, I-II, Leiden 1995–1996, I, 55–72.

J. Stackert, 2014, *A Prophet Like Moses: Prophecy, Law, and Israelite Religion*, Oxford.

M. Weinfeld, 1978, "'They Fought from Heaven' — Divine Intervention in War in Ancient Israel and in the Ancient Near East", *EI* 14, 23–30 [in Hebrew].

G. Widengren, 1970, ""What Do We Know About Moses?"", in: John I. Durham & J.R. Porter (eds.), *Proclamation and Presence; Old Testament Essays in Honour of Gwynne Henton Davies*, London, 21–47.

Y. Zakovitch, 1982, "'A Still Small Voice'", *Tarbiz* 51, 329–346 [in Hebrew].

Z. Zevit, 2009, "Deuteronomy in the Temple: An Exercise in Historical Imagining", in: N. Sacher Fox et al. (eds.), Mishneh Todah: Studies in Deuteronomy and Its Cultural Environment in Honor of Jeffrey H. Tigay, Winona Lake IN, 201–218.

CHAPTER 11

The Northern Author and the Prophetic Tent

A

One of the primary criticisms the northern author expressed was his disdain for the Golden Calf. He attacked the central religious symbol of the Israelite kingdom with his foundational story that painted the calf in a negative light (Exodus 32) as well as his regulations against making idols (Exodus 20: 18-19). A broader look at Israelite ritual during the Hebrew Biblical era shows that in addition to the calf the rites also included other symbols such as the ark and the cherubs. The ark was referred to by many names,[1] and there are a wide variety of traditions about it.

The ark began its history in the Land of Israel in the temple at Shiloh (I Samuel 1-4).[2] Afterwards it was held hostage by the Philistines during

---

[1] I will list just a few of them and their references: "The ark of God" (I Samuel 3:3, 4:14), The ark of the Lord (I Samuel 6:19), and the Ark of the covenant of the Lord" (I Kings 4:5; Jeremiah 3:16).

[2] This tradition is apparently connected to the priestly description of the establishment of the tabernacle at Shiloh (Joshua 18:1). Though the connection between this description and the history of the house of God in I Samuel:1-3 is not represented in all attested versions (for instance the Septuagint to I Samuel 2:22) however, the priestly description relies on the local tradition of the local temple, and to the contrary- the local temple tradition is dependent on its description as a divine tabernacle in non-priestly sources (Psalms 78: 60-61). Regarding the tension between the description of Shiloh as a tabernacle and a house of God, this has been discussed by the Rabbis, see Mishnah Zevahim 14:6. The affinity of the priestly tradition to Shiloh was emphasized by Haran (1962).

© The Author(s), under exclusive license to Springer Nature Switzerland AG 2024
I. Knohl, *Biblical Sinai traditions*,
https://doi.org/10.1007/978-3-031-77983-1_11

the battle of Ebenezer (I Samuel 4) and was returned to Israel after its wanderings among the Philistine cities (I Samuel 5-6). In the end it was stored in Kiriath-Yearim on the border between the Judah and Benjamin (ibid. 7:1-3), until it was brought up to Jerusalem by David (II Samuel 6), and finally into Solomon's temple (I Kings 8:1-9). The ark was significant to the general Israelite population, though it was particularly identified with the north. In the end it was appropriated by the House of David to Judah and brought to Jerusalem, so David could establish the status of his new capital.[3]

The ark was covered by the *kapôrẹt*. On top of it lay the cherubim, mythical winged creatures. Biblical Hebrew tradition considered them the focus point of the Divine presence. God is described as the One who sits above the cherubim or as hiding under their wings and revealed between them. This can be seen in the early and later strata of Biblical Hebrew composition.[4] Similarly to the ark, the general Israelite nature of this cultic

---

The deviation from the line of thinking presented here arises from our knowledge regarding the presence of the ark at Beit El and besides him Pinhas the Priest (Judges 20:27-28). Though this detail is related to other descriptions that connect Pinhas and the Ahronite priests with Beit El- such as the description of Pinhas's burial in Mt. Ephraim in Joshua 24:33 (see for instance Rofé 2009, 67–70)—it seems that this is a relatively late insertion. It interferes with the accepted order of divination in which there was a question and then an ambivalent answer (compare to I Samuel 23: 2, 4-5, 11-12). Its location shifts between the manuscripts (Masoretic Text versus the Septuagint). Above all, it raises tension regarding the priestly description in Joshua 18:1, and its remnants in the opening chapters of Samuel (compare also Judges 21:12). It separates the tabernacle and the ark and its covering, the focus of the Divine presence according to the priestly worldview (compare to Exodus 25:22). Without the ark the tabernacle is empty of presence and significance. It seems then that the item in Judges 20:27-28 was inserted by a very late scribe, an "epigone" of the priestly compositions. See Budde (1897) on the location.

[3] See Gese's discussion, 1964.

[4] Such is the case, for instance, in the northern poem in Psalms 80:2, and the priestly description of the building of the tabernacle (Exodus 25:22; and compare this to Numbers 7: 98). The fact of the cherubim as the dwelling place of God and the focus point of His presence can also be seen in the description of God, "enthroned on the cherubim" (for instance, I Samuel 4:4; II Kings 19:15) and the descriptions of God as riding a cherub (Psalms 18:11; Ezekiel 11: 22-23). In this I disagree with my student, Dr. Raanan Eichler, who suggests a different interpretation for the role of the cherubim and seeks to negate the accepted opinion that they are the seat of God (Eichler 2011; Eichler 2014). Though Eichler's works have a lot of value and contain amazing parallel materials in the ancient cultures of the Near East, I believe that it is impossible to deny the differences between the non-priestly literature which describes God sitting above the cherubim and the priestly tradi-

symbol is also clear. The importance of the cherubim is evident both in northern traditions and their Judean siblings.[5]

There is a deep connection between the ark of the covenant, the cherubim, and the tabernacle. Most of the sources note that the ark resided in the Tent of the Tabernacle before the establishment of Solomon's temple.[6] However, as mentioned, the narrative descriptions of the temple at Shiloh in I Samuel 1-4 are not sufficiently clear. On the one hand the tabernacle is referred to as a structure with a gate and doorpost (I Samuel 1:9), but on the other hand, though not attested to in all variants, the children of Eli are accused of "lay[ing] with the women who served at the entrance to the tent of meeting" (ibid. 2:22). And yet another pre-priestly source describes the temple at Shiloh as a tent, and even hints to the story of the fall of the ark and the destruction of Shiloh (Psalms 78: 60-61). Another echo of the fact that the ark resided in a tent before it was brought into Solomon's temple can be seen in Psalms 132. The text in verses 5-8 hints to the fall of Shiloh and the return of the ark to Kiriath-Yearim. "The fields of Yaar" (Verse 6) is a name for Kiriath-Yearim,[7] and the phrase "the ark of your might" is similar to the depiction of the ark in a description of the fall of Shiloh in Psalms 78 (Verse 61: "delivered his power to captivity"). In addition, Psalm 132 hints to the ark dwelling in a tent (verse 7): "Let us go to his dwelling place."[8] It is possible that this mix of tents and

---

tion according to which the cherubim cover the divine presence which is revealed between them (see, Exodus 25; 22; Leviticus 16:2; Number 7:89). These are two independent traditions each one of which has iconographic parallels in the ancient Near East.

[5] Compare the northern piece of Psalms 80:2 (you who lead Joseph like a flock! You who are enthroned upon the cherubim, shine forth), as well as the Jerusalemite Psalm 79:1 (He sits enthroned upon the cherubim; let the earth quake!), and verse 2 (The LORD is great in Zion; he is exalted over all the peoples).

[6] The identity of the tent, whether the priestly tent in Shiloh, or another tent similar that was planted by David in Jerusalem (II Smauel 6:17; 7:2), makes no difference. The main point is the idea that the ark resided in a tent, sometimes near a temple with a permanent building. See, below.

[7] See, for instance, Elitzur (2012, 248).

[8] Compare this, in the context of the site of the ark, to II Samuel 7:6; "I have been moving about in a tent and a tabernacle" as well as Psalm 78:60: "He abandoned his dwelling at Shiloh, the tent where he dwelt among mortal". See also, the picture drawn in Psalms 132:7-9 which describes the ark's journey (Verse 8: Rise up, O LORD, and go to your resting place you and the ark of your might"; and compare this to Numbers 10:35), and afterwards the promise to David (verse 10, on). This literary order fits well with the line in II Samuel 6–7. Fist the bringing of the ark, and then the promise to David in Nathan's vision. Thus, Psalms 132:7 describes a situation that takes place before the ark was brought to Jerusalem.

permanent buildings reflects reality. Societies in the process of transitioning from a nomadic lifestyle to permanent dwellings would hold on to elements of their previous ways of life. They would sometimes pitch a traditional tent next to permanent stone structures to memorialize their previous lives.[9]

There is archeological evidence of the existence of a ritual tent as it is described in Hebrew Biblical literature. The digs at the copper mines in Timna revealed a ritual tent, the remains of which were preserved thanks to the region's dry climate. Apparently, the tent was pitched by the nomads who were active in this region, the Kenites and the Midianites. Various representations of a divine presence, such as monuments and an icon of a copper snake with a golden head were discovered in the tent. At the entrance to the tent, facilities related to sacrifices were also discovered there.[10] The findings from Timna and the descriptions of the temple in Shiloh in Hebrew Biblical literature paint the picture of a similar ritual system. The rites included sacrifices, a tent, and various representations of the divine. The inanimate material findings can be augmented by the established Hebrew Biblical depiction of the priests who served at the ritual sites, like Eli and his family who performed the cult in Shiloh with the ark. This is also the case in terms of what we know regarding the worship of the calves in Beit El and Dan in which there was a priesthood and an apparatus for sacrifice within a ritual complex. Though a tent is not noted, at its center was a tangible representation of the presence of God, the calf.[11]

B

The customary Israelite ritual apparatus is an expression of a system of symbols and meanings. The ark is an expression of the permanent presence of God—"dweller among the cherubs"—in the tent. The priests serve the permanent divine resident. They regularly offer sacrifices and

---

[9] This can be seen in the modern era in the Bedouin settlements in the Negev.

[10] For a description of the findings see Avner (2014).

[11] Of course, the entirety of ritual and symbolic worship is reflected in the priestly tradition in which the tent of the tabernacle included an ark, candelabra, table, etc. Perhaps this tradition reflects the foundations of the cult and ancient customs, since its primary details are identical to what has been described in the pre-priestly traditions and non-Hebrew Biblical sources. See also my note above regarding the connection between the descriptions of the temple in Shiloh to the priestly tradition of the tent of the tabernacle as it settled in this place.

maintain the site, like one who serves a resident their meals and attends to the needs of the house.[12] The text, however, blatantly and clearly rejects anthropomorphizing God, as was done in neighboring cultures that believed that their god lived in a shrine and was nourished by sacrifices.[13] That being said the picture that arises from Hebrew Biblical literature preserves remnants of the ritual apparatus as it is expressed in archeological findings and non-Hebrew Biblical parallels.

Here we can note another aspect of the northern author's revolution: In the face of the ancient tradition regarding the ritual tent, reflected in Timna and Shiloh, he suggests an entirely different model for the role of the tent.[14] His position is first reflected in the description of the establishment of the tent by Moses after the sin of the Golden Calf (Exodus 33:7-11):

Now Moses used to take the tent and pitch it outside the camp, far off from the camp; he called it the tent of meeting. And everyone who sought the LORD would go out to the tent of meeting, which was outside the camp. 8 Whenever Moses went out to the tent, all the people would rise and stand, each of them, at the entrance of their tents and watch Moses until he had gone into the tent. When Moses entered the tent, the pillar of cloud would descend and stand at the entrance of the tent, and the LORD[b] would speak with Moses. 10 When all the people saw the pillar of cloud standing at the entrance of the tent, all the people would rise and bow down, all of them, at the entrance of their tent. 11 Thus the LORD used to speak to Moses face to face, as one speaks to a friend. Then he would return to the camp, but his young assistant, Joshua son of Nun, would not leave the tent.

[12] The picture of the contents of the tent is richer in the priestly literature in the Torah: It contains, among other things, a candelabra for light, a table for the showbread, as is necessary for God to live in the place. Though, in terms of the narrative, it is later than the pre-priestly layers of the Torah, there is no reason to think that it does not reflect reality and early customs. It is natural that the priestly circles would draw a rich and more detailed picture of the organization of the temple, even if those ideas were expressed outside those circles at a later stage in the history of the literature. The idea of the Divine presence as represented in priestly literature and the implementation of those ideas is another issue. See below.

[13] See Knohl (1995, 128–137).

[14] The discussion here is based on an article I wrote in honor of my late teacher Professor M. Greenberg. See Knohl (1997).

This tent is different from the other priestly tent described in the Torah as well as from the tents described in pre-priestly materials in the early prophets. As opposed to the priestly tent, it is located outside of the camp. Likewise, as opposed to the rest of the tents, this tent is empty and does not contain a tangible representation of the presence of God in the form of the ark or cherubim (or the monuments and icons of the sorts found in Timna). Just the reverse is true, it seems that God was not permanently present in the tent, but appeared at the opening of the tent in a pillar of smoke for a limited time when Moses was in the tent. The cloud would depart when Moses returned to the camp (verse 9:11, as well as Numbers 12:9-10). In this tent there were also no sacrifices or priesthood, which are dependent, as mentioned above, on the permanent presence of God and the obligation to serve Him. Moses's servant, Joshua, was the only one who permanently resided in the tent: "but his young assistant, Joshua son of Nun, would not leave the tent" (Exodus 33:11).

Joshua of Ephraim, as mentioned, was not a priest, and according to the priestly legislation in the Torah, would not be allowed to enter the tent of the tabernacle at all, since he was not of the tribe of Levi (Numbers 3:10). And yet, the northern author's tent was open to all (Exodus 33:7): "And everyone who sought the LORD would go out to the tent of meeting, which was outside the camp". The phrase "sought the Lord" is obtuse, and it is not clear whether it refers to prayer or the request for a prophetic sign or question.[15] Either way the tent was open to all and egalitarian in nature. It did not have a priesthood or a hierarchy of holiness, and lay people were allowed to enter it. It was, then, entirely different from the priestly tent of the tabernacle, and in a similar manner, from the early traditions regarding the tent and the ark described in the other sources.

This suits the revolutionary world view of the northern author described above. He sees in all of Israel "a priestly kingdom and a holy nation" (Exodus 19:6) and demands of them to be "people consecrated to me" (22:30). He had demonstrated his position with the covenant ceremony in which the youth of Israel—and not a separate Levitical priesthood!—brought sacrifices (Exodus 24:5). So, the northern author also described the tent of the tabernacle in keeping with his rejection of an institutionalized priesthood as can be seen in the other texts that he composed. This

---

[15] For the first possibility, see for instance, Propp, Exodus, vol. II, 600; for the second-Driver (1911, 359).

also suits the lack of priests and the lack of prominence of the tribe of Levi in the northern author's compositions. Moses and Aaron are not described as being from the tribe of Levi or as priests in his works. The revolutionary egalitarianism that the northern author imposed on the rites was not limited to legislation and sacrificial worship alone, but also exists in the characteristics of revelation itself.

It is in this context that scholars have noted the similarities between the prophetic tent and the description of the revelation at Horeb in the northern author's composition.[16] During the event in Horeb, it says: "Moses brought the people out of the camp to meet God. They took their stand at the foot of the mountain." (Exodus 19: 17). Similarly, the prophetic tent of the tabernacle is also set up outside of the camp and Moses and all those who seek God go out to it. During the event at Horeb God appears in a cloud above the mountain and speaks to Moses. The revelation occurs in full sight of the people and its purpose is to establish Moses's leadership (Exodus 19:9): "I am going to come to you in a dense cloud, in order that the people may hear when I speak with you and so trust you ever after." The development of the event as is described also has similar characteristics to that of the revelation at the tent at the tabernacle. God reveals Himself in a cloud on the mountain and speaks with Moses in the presence of the nation (Exodus 19:16-19), just as at the tent God reveals Himself to Moses in a cloud and speaks with him in the presence of the nation (Exodus 33:9).

The similarities between the events at Horeb and the establishment of the tent of the tabernacle indicate both continuity and development. The event at Horeb was a one-time revelation that ended in the sin of the Golden Calf and the cancellation of the covenant. However, the northern author saw this as a temporary crisis that was resolved with the establishment of the tent of the tabernacle, a tool for permanent and continuous revelation. The connection between God and His people was not broken. Moses's authority was not at all harmed by the crisis. Just the reverse is true, the connection between him and God remained and became more frequent, as well as the nation's ability to witness it. In this sense, the tent of the tabernacle continuously renews the events of Horeb, the covenant with God, and Moses's authority. At the same time, the figure of Joshua is strengthened. He is Moses's attendant (Exodus 24:13; 32:17) who permanently dwells in the Tent (Exodus 32:11). He descends from the

---

[16] Haran (1956, 15–16). For other scholars see, Seri-Levi (2020, 167, footnote 143).

northern tribe, Ephraim and his appointment as Moses's successor rein-
forces the theory that the composition before us is indeed northern
in origin.

The figure of Joshua is another connection between the events at
Horeb, the Golden Calf, and the erection of the prophetic tent. He
accompanies Moses when he goes up on to the mountain (Exodus 24:13).
He stays there until Moses returns and returns with him to the camp that
is embroiled in the worship of the Golden Calf (Exodus 32:17). Afterwards,
it is indeed Joshua who accompanies Moses in erecting the outer tent and
stays there permanently (Exodus 32:11), including during the prophesizing of the elders and the deeds of Eldad and Medad (Numbers 11:28). In
the end, Moses and Joshua are called to the tent where the attendant is
appointed to inherit the role of his master (Deut. 31:14-15).[17]

So, the northern author's revolution was not limited to attacking the
worship of the calves in the northern kingdom. He also declared war
against the general Israelite conception of a ritual space in which there is a
tent and physical representations of the constant presence of God, whether
it was an ark, cherubim, or calves. He exchanged those traditional symbols
with the tent of the tabernacle outside the camp. With this the northern
author did indeed retain something of the ancient tradition, but it is only
the trappings of something completely different: the tent empty of an ark
or cherubim, without sacrifices, a priesthood, or a hierarchy of holiness.
God is not present there permanently. This is a new version of Israelite
religious symbols.

C

In another context, I theorized that the northern author sought to reject
the idea about the permanent presence of God on earth.[18] According to
him, God is not present on earth permanently and does not live among
Israel but rather in heaven. He reveals Himself for a little while in a pillar
of cloud at the opening of the tent. Afterwards, He returns to His dwell-

---

[17] I have noted above, in keeping with my predecessors (see above Chap. 9), the similarities
between the northern author's composition and the traditions regarding Elijah and Elisha
and the circles of the sons of the prophets in which they developed. It seems that Joshua's
inheritance of Moses's role parallels to the relationship between Elijah and Elisha. See spe-
cially the way a student inherits the role of the master (Num. 27:15-23; Deut. 31:14-23; I
Kings 19:21; II Kings 2:1-15).

[18] See Knohl (1995, 131 and footnote 24), as well as Knohl (1997).

ing in heaven.[19] This position argued, as mentioned, for the revocation of the priesthood. Given the lack of a permanent Divine presence in a particular residence, the entire cultic complex loses its meaning. If the resident is not in His house, who is there left to serve? The northern author's theological understanding has practical implications for social and religious institutions.

Naturally, the revocation of the priesthood and making the holiest places accessible to lay people paint a picture of a more egalitarian society than the one rejected by the northern author. This can be seen above in our author's cultic regulations. He advocated for simple ritual, lacking glory, in which everyone is allowed to serve in the holiest places.[20] Where did the northern author get his tendency towards egalitarianism? We have discussed the place of our author in the cultural stream that was active during the last generations of the northern kingdom. This stream disdained the monarchy and sharply criticized the corruption of northern society. There is even a sense of nostalgia for the pre-monarchical era- for the days of the judges. It is possible that there is some support for this nostalgic picture. An analysis of the archeological finds from the Bronze Age I Israelite settlements shows that they had a tendency towards simplicity and egalitarianism. For instance, though there are scattered examples of material opulence, such as the adorned and colorful Philistine ceramics, these are not found in Israelite sites. Though Israelite society surely changed over the generations, it's possible that something of their ancient tendency was preserved, at least among certain streams of thought. Given the lack of additional findings this can only remain a theory.[21]

However, at least from a narrative perspective one can find a connecting thread between the northern author's worldview and the northern literary traditions regarding the end of the settlement period and the beginning of the monarchy. The sources regarding this period describe Samuel the Prophet and the group of prophets around him (I Samuel19: 18-24). In specific, the description of Saul prophesizing within the band of prophets (I Samuel 10: 5-6, 10-13) reflects this. In addition, Samuel resided in Naioth in Ramah (I Samuel 19:19). Apparently, the Naioth were tents

---

[19] This was developed in a similar manner by Seri-Levi (2020, 163), etc. This can also be seen in the northern author's ritual legislation. God appears near earthen and stone altars temporarily when His name is mentioned (Exodus 20:21). There is no permanent presence of God at the given location.

[20] See above, Chap. 8.

[21] Faust (2013).

that were erected at the edges of the town of Ramah, the place where Samuel and his followers, the prophesiers lived.[22]

There is a clear similarity between these traditions regarding the tent of the prophets and the prophetic tent that Moses erected according to the northern author. The tents are not in a private closed area. At their center is a prophet. Other prophesiers, lower than him in hierarchy and even subordinate to him, surround him. This arrangement can especially be seen in the description of Moses's tent in Numbers 12:16-17, 24-30 as the place where the seventy elders prophesized under the supervision of Moses. The desert description might reflect the tradition about Samuel's generation.[23]

On the other hand, the glorification of Moses arouses tension relative to the northern author's egalitarian vision of society, and the service of God, including prophecy. However, the story of Eldad and Medad prophesying in the camp reveals a continuation of his egalitarian trend. Moses's words, "would that all the Lord's people were prophets" (Numbers 11:29), can be connected to the northern author's statement during the revelation at Horeb regarding "a priestly kingdom and holy nation" (Exodus 19:6), and "you shall be a people consecrated to Me", (Exodus 22:30). And yet, the next description of the prophetic tent places Moses on a higher level than the rest of the prophets who were active in Israel; in this context- Aharon and Miriam (Numbers 12:1-13, and 6-8):[24]

---

[22] Regarding Naioth as the plural of *nāwę*, which became *nāwôt* see the entry in HALOT, *nāwę*, It is possible that the form here was a copyist's mistake (which is reflected in the qeri and ketiv), and the original form was נוה which is preserved in Zephania 2:6. Regarding *nāwę* as a tent see the parallels in Isaiah 33, as well as the description in II Samuel 7:8, which reflects a shepherding society in which tents were common. In addition, the term *nāwę* is attested in an ancient form already in the Mari Documents where it describes a camp of semi-nomadic people. See Malamat (1962, 146). Regarding the fact that the tents of Naioth of Ramah were outside the city, see the Medieval commentator Radak: "or this was a place outside of the city called Ramah, close to it, within its borders".

[23] Regarding the similarity and closeness between the tradition of the prophetic tent and the description of the prophesiers at the start of the monarchy, see Noth, **Numbers**, 89; Jenks (1977, 89–91), Stackert (2014, 100–102).

[24] Regarding the prophecy of Aharon and Miriam compare (Micah 6:4). I tend to agree with Stackert's opinion (2014, 70–125), that the northern author sought to restrict the authority and status of the prophets of his generation such as Amos and Hosea.

When there are prophets among you,
  I the LORD make myself known to them in visions;
  I speak to them in dreams.
7 Not so with my servant Moses;
  he is faithful in all my house.
8 With him I speak face to face—clearly, not in riddles,

Even the northern author's revolution had limits. Moses's prophecy was something that could be aspired to, but not reached.

D

Julius Wellhausen saw the cultic patterns of the non-priestly sources in the Torah as an expression of the free spirit of the early Israelites, the young, spontaneous, natural, and non-institutionalized generation.[25] In contrast, I argue that the northern author, who is one of the non-priestly authors referred to by Wellhausen, worked against the institutions and the opulent ritual symbols and practices that already existed in the kingdoms of Judah and Israel for hundreds of years. The ritual system presented by the northern author rejects those ritual symbols and acts, and instead establishes a picture of egalitarian simple ritual, open to everyone. There is room to assume that the northern author's revolution drew from sources and (pre) narrative traditions that existed at the dawn of the Israelite society before the establishment of the monarchy.

BIBLIOGRAPHY

U. Avner, 2014, "Egyptian Timna — Reconsiderd", in: J.M. Tebes (ed.), *Unearthing the Wilderness: Studies on the History and Archaeology of the Negev and Edom in the Iron Age* (Ancient Near Eastern Studies Supp. 45), Leuven-Paris-Walpole MA, 103–162.

K. Budde, 1897, *Das Buch der Richter* (KHC), Freiburg-Leipzig-Tübingen.

S.R. Driver, 1911, *Exodus* (CB), Cambridge.

R. Eichler, 2011, "The Function of the Ark Cherubim", *Tarbiz* 79, 165–185 [in Hebrew].

R. Eichler, 2014, "The Meaning of יֹשֵׁב הַכְּרֻבִים", *ZAW* 126, 358–371.

---

[25] He demonstrates this via various elements of the ritual as they are seen in the sources and legal collections in the Torah: Wellhausen, **Prolegomena**, 19-167.

Y. Elitzur, 2012, *Ancient Toponyms in the Land of Israel: Preservation and History* (2nd ed.), Jerusalem [in Hebrew].

A. Faust, 2013, "Early Israel: An Egalitarian Society", *BAR* 39/4, 45–49.

H. Gese, 1964, "Der Davidsbund und die Zionserwählung", *ZTK* 61, 10–26.

M. Haran, 1956, "The Tent of Meeting", *Tarbiz* 25, 11–20 [in Hebrew].

M. Haran, 1962, "Shiloh and Jerusalem: The Origin of the Priestly Tradition in the Pentateuch", *JBL* 81, 14–24.

A. Jenks, 1977, *The Elohist and the North Israelite Traditions* (SBLMS 22), Missoula MT.

I. Knohl, 1995, *The Sanctuary of Silence: The Priestly Torah and the Holiness School*, Minneapolis.

I. Knohl, 1997, "Two Aspects of the 'Tent of Meeting'", in: M. Cogan et al. (eds.), *Tehila le-Moshe (Fs. M. Greenberg)*, Winona Lake IN, 73–78.

A. Malamat, 1962, "Mari and the Bible: Some Patterns of Tribal Organization and Institutions", *JAOS* 82, 143–150.

A. Rofé, 2009, *Introduction to the Literature of the Hebrew Bible*, Jerusalem.

Seri Levi, 2020, א' סרי־לוי, הכעס האלוהי והדרכים לשיכוכו בתורה ובמקורותיה (דיסרטציה), ירושלים. A. Seri – Levi, Divine Anger and its Appeasement, Dissertation, The Hebrew University.

J. Stackert, 2014, *A Prophet Like Moses: Prophecy, Law, and Israelite Religion*, Oxford.

CHAPTER 12

Conclusion

The northern author appeared at a crucial turning point in the world of Hebrew Biblical prophecy. The ancient prophecy that had flourished under the influence of miracle workers such as Samuel, Elijah, and Elisha, and in which group prophecy and ecstasy were common, began to decline. It was pushed aside by the classic written prophecy starting around the middle of the eighth century BCE. This type of prophecy was centered around a single prophet who was not necessarily surrounded by a group of followers and students.[1]

The appearance of the literary prophets was, as mentioned, part of the transition from an entirely oral culture to a culture in which writing was beginning to take a central role. The northern author and his works were part of this turning point. However, this author is distinct from the literary prophets in his genre of literature. The literary prophets expressed themselves in the same genre as did the ancient Hebrew poets, poetry.[2] The northern author abandoned poetics and took up a prose.

One can only guess what motivated the anonymous northern author to choose as he did. I believe that this process reflects his target audience. Naturally, poetry is written in high and flowery language, which is only

---

[1] Regarding the change in the status of the prophet as well as the attitude towards prophets see, for instance, Uffenheimer (2001, 28–41); Rofé (1988, 97–99).

[2] This can be seen in parallelisms, which is the primary characteristic of Hebrew Biblical poetry, as well as the poetry of neighboring cultures, see Kugel (2011).

© The Author(s), under exclusive license to Springer Nature Switzerland AG 2024
I. Knohl, *Biblical Sinai traditions*,
https://doi.org/10.1007/978-3-031-77983-1_12

understandable to those chosen educated individuals. The tidings of cooperation and egalitarianism of the northern author was meant for the masses, and clear and understandable language was needed for lay people to be able to grasp. And indeed, his narrative style is clear, sharp, and in keeping with this, easily comprehensible.

* * *

Previously proponents of the schola of Hebrew Bible criticism found that the Torah was composed of several sources, including E, also known as the Elohistic source. This source is essentially congruent with what I have called until now the "northern author". The status of the documentary hypothesis has been declining since the 1970s. The recognition of the very existence of the Elohistic source is in doubt. Its place was taken, mostly in European research, by theories that negate the existence of continuous sources throughout the Torah and give preference to independent traditions surrounding events or central figures in the text.[3]

I strove not to obligate myself to either theory, since both theories can go well in terms of our subject. In terms of the documentary hypothesis one can see my book as a comparison between the ancient poetry and the Elohistic version of the giving of the laws at Horeb and the sin of the Golden Calf. To those who reject the documentary hypothesis I can say that this book is a comparison between ancient poetry and the early narrative strata related to the story of revelation at Mt. Horeb-Sinai. The characterization of this narrative strata as northern in origin, and as work of itself, is not dependent on any one of the theories or their assumptions.[4]

---

[3] For a clear presentation of the documentary hypothesis see Friedman, Torah; Schwartz (2021). See also the analysis of the sources in the Horeb story by Schwartz (1997, 2009). Regarding the theories which reject the documentary hypothesis as well as current trends in research see the surveys by Van Seters (1999, 20–86); Römer (2013); Albertz (2018).

[4] In another place, I noted the tension between the story of the revelation to Jacob at Beth El, (Genesis 28:10-22), which is essentially an E story, and the descriptions of the prophetic tent of the tabernacle in Exodus and Numbers (Knohl 2003, 77–82). In addition, I have not found any reference to the stories of the patriarchs in the texts that I attribute to the northern author in this monograph. So, my current arguments could go hand in hand with Conrad Schmid's theory regarding the separate origins of the story of the Patriarchs and the stories of Moses, the exodus from Egypt and the wanderings in the desert (Schmid 2010). Meaning, his theory and my arguments, do not necessarily negate each other. In any case, the analysis suggested here, is not dependent on any theory, notations or tags that were created to separate the texts and sources.

As mentioned, the northern author was probably active in the Israelite kingdom in the middle of the eighth century BCE. Not long afterwards, the kingdom was destroyed and many of its residents were exiled by the Assyrians. Luckily enough the northern author's work survived by making its way southward to the Kingdom of Judah. As is well known, Jerusalem's sudden and swift growth at the last third of the eighth century BCE can best be explained by the arrival and absorption of a wave of refugees from the northern kingdom. Though it is possible that there are other reasons for the growth of the city at this time, it is reasonable to assume that this process stemmed mainly from population migration from the destroyed northern kingdom.[5] It is also possible that the journey of the northern composition southward happened in stages: first from the center in Samaria, to Benjamin, which was not conquered by the Assyrians, on the border of Judah, and from there to Jerusalem.[6]

*   *   *

The acceptance of the northern author in Judah led to the continuation and further development of the narrative about the composition about the Sinai—Horeb revelation with the figure of Moses the prophet and legislator at its center in the coming generations. This process was accompanied with the suppression and silencing of the ancient poetic traditions. However, the broken mosaic tiles of ancient poetry were not discarded or

---

[5] See Broshi (1974). There has been opposition to this theory over the last few generations. The most prominent critic is Nadav Na'aman (see for instance, Na'aman 2007, 2014; see also Guillaume 2008). However, I do not agree with him. He does not establish a persuasive explanation for the sudden and exceptional growth in Jerusalem's size. Refugees from the plains who escaped the threat of the Assyrian armies are not a solution to this puzzle. The discovery of the "broad wall" and the houses built on top of them show that the city's expansion to the western hill as well as its encapsulation by a wall occurred before the Assyrian assault (compare to Isaiah 22:1). In addition, the very fact of the existence of laws regarding returning escapees and deserters in legal documents and contracts, as well as in royal inscriptions in the ancient near east, show that refugees existed and that rulers sought to manage this phenomenon. Meaning, there is nothing to negate the idea of Israelites fleeing to Judah, just the reverse is true. In addition, the transfer of the northern tradition southward is not dependent on a large stream of refugees. All that is needed are a few educated individuals carrying documents and a few scrolls. See also, Finkelstein's response, 2008.

[6] Regarding Benjamin as a cultural and spiritual mediator between the north and south, see Knauf (2006); Davies (2007); Na'aman (2009), and Chap. 6, section 2, above. Information regarding figures from Benjamin living in Jerusalem should also be considered. The most prominent of them was Jeremiah, the prophet from Anathoth. See also, Jeremiah 6:1.

entirely removed from the Hebrew Biblical collection. Thanks to this, contemporary scholars of the Hebrew Bible can collect them and piece them together to clearly look anew at this ancient and shining image.

*   *   *

As mentioned, it was the revolutionary northern author who first established the figure of Moses as a legislator who mediated between God and Israel and placed him at the heart of the Hebrew Biblical composition, and Jewish tradition in general. It is he who took the ancient poems and adapted and reedited the separate elements of those poems. In doing so he created, for the first time, a picture of the event at Mt. Horeb or Sinai, an event that begins with a public revelation to the whole nation and continues with the transmission of a book of laws to Moses in a unique and private manner.

Placing Moses the Prophet at the center of the story of revelation at Horeb-Sinai changed the character of Hebrew Biblical religion. Before the activity of the northern author, Israelite religion did not rely upon the figure of the prophet-legislator. In the earlier stages of its evolution, as is reflected in poems created before the eighth century BCE, Biblical Hebrew religion was not a "prophetic religion". The early prophets such as Samuel or Elijah, did not have an established religious role. They worked as preservers and supporters of the Israelite faith at times of crisis but did not have the status of founders of the faith or religion. It is only after the works of the northern author and the other Torah authors who followed in his footsteps, that the new portrait of the Israelite faith and Judaism come into being. It is from there that it grew as a prophetic religion reliant on the figure of Moses and his decisive role as the mediator of Divine revelation to the nation of Israel.

BIBLIOGRAPHY

R. Albertz, 2018, "The Recent Discussion on the Formation of the Pentateuch/ Hexateuch", *Hebrew Studies* 59, 65–92.

M. Broshi, 1974, "The Expansion of Jerusalem in the Reigns of Hezekiah and Manasseh", *IEJ* 24, 21–26.

P.R. Davies, 2007, "The Trouble with Benjamin", in: R. Rezetko et al. (eds.), *Reflection and Refraction (Fs. A.G. Auld)* (SVT 113), Leiden, 93–111.

Israel Finkelstein, 2008, "The Settlement History of Jerusalem in the Eighth and Seventh Centuries BC", *RB* 115, 499–515.

P. Guillaume, 2008, "Jerusalem 720-705 BCE. No Flood of Israelite Refugees", *SJOT* 22, 195–211.

E.A. Knauf, 2006, "Bethel: The Israelite Impact on Judean Language and Literature", in: O. Lipschits and M. Oeming (ed.), *Judah and the Judeans in the Persian Period*, Winona Lake IN, 291–350.

I. Knohl, 2003, *The Divine Symphony: The Bible's Many Voices*, Philadelphia PA.

J. L. Kugel, 2011, "Biblical Poetry", in: Z. Talshir et al. (eds.) *The Literature of the Hebrew Bible*, Yad Ben-Zvi Press, Jerusalem, 3–36.

N. Na'aman, 2007, "When and How Did Jerusalem Become a Great City? The Rise of Jerusalem as Judah's Premier City in the Eighth-Seventh Centuries B.C.E.", *BASOR* 347, 21–56.

N. Na'aman, 2009, "Saul, Benjamin and the Emergence of 'Biblical Israel'", *ZAW* 121, 211–224, 335–349.

N. Na'aman, 2014, "Dismissing the Myth of a Flood of Israelite Refugees in the Late Eighth Century BCE", *ZAW* 126, 1–14.

A. Rofé, 1988, *The Prophetical Stories: The Narratives About the Prophets in the Hebrew Bible, Their Literary Types and History*, Jerusalem.

T. Römer, 2013, "Zwischen Urkunden, Fragmenten und Ergänzungen: Zum Stand der Pentateuchforschung", *ZAW* 125, 2–24.

K. Schmid, 2010, *Genesis and the Moses Story: Israel's Dual Origins in the Hebrew Bible* (Eng. Transl. by J.D. Nogalski), Winona Lake IN.

B. J. Schwartz, "What Really Happened at Mount Sinai?", *BR* (October 1997), 21–46.

B.J. Schwartz, 2009, "The Visit of Jethro: A Case of Chronological Displacement? The Source-Critical Solution", in: N.S. Fox et al. (eds.), *Mishneh Todah: Studies in Deuteronomy and Its Cultural Environment in Honor of Jeffery H. Tigay*, Winona Lake IN, 29–48.

B.J. Schwartz, 2021, "The Documentary Hypothesis", in: J.S. Baden and J. Stackert (eds.), *The Oxford Handbook of the Pentateuch*, Oxford, 165–187.

B. Uffenheimer, 2001, *Classical Prophecy: The Prophetic Consciousness*, Jerusalem [in Hebrew].

J. Van Seters, 1999, *The Pentateuch: A Social-Science Commentary*, London – New York NY.

Appendix A: Wellhausen's Theory About the Revelation at Kadesh and Its Refutation

The theory that the Torah contains an alternative, divergent tradition regarding the location of the giving of the laws and commandments had already been posited by Wellhausen. He and his followers saw Kadesh, or Kadesh Barnea as the place of revelation. In this way he opened the door for various theories regarding the status of Kadesh in ancient times.[1]

The weakness of Wellhausen's argument is in the establishment of Kadesh as the location of the revelation and the giving of the laws. It relies on unreliable readings of the texts that were inserted into the description of the appearance of God at the beginning of Moses's Blessings (Deut. 33, 1-5). The most prominent of those readings is the phrase, *meribebot qodeš* "myriads of holy ones" (33:2). Wellhausen read the text as *meribat qadeš* since it is the last phrase in a list of geographic locations (Sinai-Seir-Paran). This edit was made according to the well-known phrase מריבת קדש in the priestly strata of the Torah (see for instance, Numbers 27; 14; Deut. 32, 51), as well as the description of the borders of the Land of Israel in Ezekiel 47: 13-20 (verses 19, 48, 28).[2] In keeping with this, Wellhausen identified all the locations in which the words tests, or *meribah* at Kadesh appear with an alternative tradition to the one regarding Sinai-Horeb.

---

[1] See Wellhausen, **Prolegomena**, 342–347. See, in a similar vein, Gressmann (1913, 419–424, 431ff.).

[2] A similar edit was suggested by Dillmann (1886, 417): "*woʾātâ memeribat qadeš*".

I. Knohl, *Biblical Sinai traditions*, https://doi.org/10.1007/978-3-031-77983-1

According to Wellhaussen, this tradition believed that law was given to Israel at Kadesh.

Though these days it seems that the strength of this theory has waned, the very fact of a theory that is similar in spirit to my own, obligates us to address Wellhausen's suggestion.[3] As others have noted, there is a fundamental flaw at the foundation of his theory. The poem in Deuteronomy 33 is an ancient northern composition. It is natural that it would be full of difficult phrases and errors due to its age and complicated transmission. Wellhausen preferred to edit the text in light of the late priestly phrase "*mê meriḇat qaḏēš*".[4] The edit does not take into account the ancient language in a similar description in Psalms 68:18: "רכב אלהים רבתים אלפי שנאן". God is described here surrounded by an army of thousands of angels. This description is similar to the Masoretic version of Deuteronomy 33, 2 *meriḇebot qoḏēš* . The similarly between the two poems and Psalms 68 and Deuteronomy 33 and their essential early date, give a preference to the interpretation of the text in Deut. 33, 2 considering the text in the ancient psalm. Moses's poem describes the appearance of God. It is natural that His angels would also be represented during His journey.[5]

Another weakness in Wellhausen's Kadesh theory can be found in the way he dealt with the other sources that were attributed to it. The theory paints all mentions of Kadesh and Massah and Meribah with one brush without taking into account the difference between the texts and the tradition's lack of consolidation and gradual development. In my opinion, one must distinguish between the descriptions in which God is the one who tests His nation and those in which it is the nation that tests their God. The texts of the first kind (Deut. 33:8; Psalms 71:8) are northern in origin and touch upon the preservation of the covenant and the prohibition against idol worship. On the other hand, the texts regarding the nation's rebellion and their testing of God touch upon the provisions of food and water in the desert. The earlier expressions of this tradition can be found in Psalms 78:18-20. However, while this Judean source (see 78:60-72) does indeed note the test that the nation tested God with while in the desert (ibid. 18), it does not mention Massah or Meribah at all. A secondary Judean edit combined the northern traditions with its own

---

[3] Regarding the abandonment of Wellhausen's Kadesh hypothesis see the encyclopedia entries by Schipper (2008, 3) and Jericke (2020).
[4] See Seligmann's doubts, (1964, 191); Propp (1987, 73).
[5] See a similar suggestion by Mayes (1979, 399 ad loc).

sources and connected Massah and Meribah to the Israelite's complaints in the desert. This action was part of the broader process that we described above regarding the transposition of the location of the revelation and the giving of the laws from the waters of Meribah to Horeb. In this way the tradition regarding the waters of Meribah was emptied of its primary content- God's testing of Israel in the context of the prohibition against serving foreign gods—and a different test took its place: the nation tested God regarding the provision of Israel's needs in the desert.[6]

[6] A tradition that stands on its own right is reflected in Psalm 95. According to this psalm it was Israel that tested God at Meribah "On the day of Massah in the desert" Psalms 95:5. The exact nature of the test is not elaborated on in the text. This brought about the punishment of forty years of wandering in the desert and death before entering the Land of Israel (*vv.* 10-11).

APPENDIX B: THE REVELATION OF THE LAW AND THE GOLDEN CALF IN THE NORTHERN NARRATIVE

The Revelation:[1]
Exod.19
[2] And when they set out from Reph'idim and came into the wilderness of Sinai, they encamped in the wilderness; and there Israel encamped before the mountain.

[3] And Moses went up to God, and the LORD called to him out of the mountain, saying, "Thus you shall say to the house of Jacob, and tell the people of Israel:

[4] You have seen what I did to the Egyptians, and how I bore you on eagles' wings and brought you to myself.

[5] Now therefore, if you will obey my voice and keep my covenant, you shall be my own possession among all peoples; for all the earth is mine,

[6] and you shall be to me a kingdom of priests and a holy nation. These are the words which you shall speak to the children of Israel."

---

[1] The division presented in this appendix is similar to the divisions suggested by Baden (2012, 117) etc., Stackert (2014, 75–97). Except for a few places (see the next note), their division is not majorly different than the one presented here. For a division of the sources in Exodus 19 see Schwartz (1997). According to this division, which I accept, the verses in Exodus 19: 9b-15, as well as the words, "on the morning of the third day", (19:16a), belong to the J document. As Seri-Levi recently pointed out (in press) the continuation of verse 16 which describes the vocal characteristics of the mountain, is also from document J. I want to thank Dr. Seri-Levi for providing me with a copy of their article which has not yet been published.

© The Author(s), under exclusive license to Springer Nature Switzerland AG 2024
I. Knohl, *Biblical Sinai traditions*,
https://doi.org/10.1007/978-3-031-77983-1

119

[7]
So Moses came and called the elders of the people, and set before them all these words which the LORD had commanded him.

[8] And all the people answered together and said, "All that the LORD has spoken we will do." And Moses reported the words of the people to the LORD.

[9] And the LORD said to Moses, "Lo, I am coming to you in a thick cloud, that the people may hear when I speak with you, and may also believe you for ever."

[17] Then Moses brought the people out of the camp to meet God; and they took their stand at the foot of the mountain.

[19] And as the sound of the trumpet grew louder and louder, Moses spoke, and God answered him in thunder.

Exod.20

[1]
And God spoke all these words, saying,

[2] "I am the LORD your God, who brought you out of the land of Egypt, out of the house of bondage.

[3]
"You shall have no other gods before me.

[4]
"You shall not make for yourself a graven image, or any likeness of any-thing that is in heaven above, or that is in the earth beneath, or that is in the water under the earth;

[5] you shall not bow down to them or serve them; for I the LORD your God am a jealous God, visiting the iniquity of the fathers upon the children to the third and the fourth generation of those who hate me,

[6] but showing steadfast love to thousands of those who love me and keep my commandments.

[7]
"You shall not take the name of the LORD your God in vain; for the LORD will not hold him guiltless who takes his name in vain.

[8]
"Remember the sabbath day, to keep it holy.

[9] Six days you shall labor, and do all your work;

[10] but the seventh day is a sabbath to the LORD your God; in it you shall not do any work, you, or your son, or your daughter, your manser-vant, or your maidservant, or your cattle, or the sojourner who is within your gates;

[11] for in six days the LORD made heaven and earth, the sea, and all that is in them, and rested the seventh day; therefore the LORD blessed the sabbath day and hallowed it.

[12]
"Honor your father and your mother, that your days may be long in the land which the LORD your God gives you.

[13]
"You shall not kill.

[14]
"You shall not commit adultery.

[15]
"You shall not steal.

[16]
"You shall not bear false witness against your neighbor.

[17]
"You shall not covet your neighbor's house; you shall not covet your neighbor's wife, or his manservant, or his maidservant, or his ox, or his ass, or anything that is your neighbor's."

[18]
Now when all the people perceived the thunderings and the lightnings and the sound of the trumpet and the mountain smoking, the people were afraid and trembled; and they stood afar off,

[19] and said to Moses, "You speak to us, and we will hear; but let not God speak to us, lest we die."

[20] And Moses said to the people, "Do not fear; for God has come to prove you, and that the fear of him may be before your eyes, that you may not sin."

[21]
And the people stood afar off, while Moses drew near to the thick darkness where God was.

[22] And the LORD said to Moses, "Thus you shall say to the people of Israel: 'You have seen for yourselves that I have talked with you from heaven.

[23] You shall not make gods of silver to be with me, nor shall you make for yourselves gods of gold.

[24] An altar of earth you shall make for me and sacrifice on it your burnt offerings and your peace offerings, your sheep and your oxen; in every place where I cause my name to be remembered I will come to you and bless you.

[25] And if you make me an altar of stone, you shall not build it of hewn stones; for if you wield your tool upon it you profane it.

[26] And you shall not go up by steps to my altar, that your nakedness be not exposed on it.'

[26] And you shall not go up by steps to my altar, that your nakedness be not exposed on it.'

Exod.21

[1]

"Now these are the ordinances which you shall set before them.

[2] When you buy a Hebrew slave, he shall serve six years, and in the seventh he shall go out free, for nothing.

[3] If he comes in single, he shall go out single; if he comes in married, then his wife shall go out with him.

[4] If his master gives him a wife and she bears him sons or daughters, the wife and her children shall be her master's and he shall go out alone.

[5] But if the slave plainly says, 'I love my master, my wife, and my children; I will not go out free,'

[6] then his master shall bring him to God, and he shall bring him to the door or the doorpost; and his master shall bore his ear through with an awl; and he shall serve him for life.

[7]

"When a man sells his daughter as a slave, she shall not go out as the male slaves do.

[8] If she does not please her master, who has designated her for himself, then he shall let her be redeemed; he shall have no right to sell her to a foreign people, since he has dealt faithlessly with her.

[9] If he designates her for his son, he shall deal with her as with a daughter.

[10] If he takes another wife to himself, he shall not diminish her food, her clothing, or her marital rights.

[11] And if he does not do these three things for her, she shall go out for nothing, without payment of money.

[12]

"Whoever strikes a man so that he dies shall be put to death.

[13] But if he did not lie in wait for him, but God let him fall into his hand, then I will appoint for you a place to which he may flee.

[14] But if a man willfully attacks another to kill him treacherously, you shall take him from my altar, that he may die.

[15]
"Whoever strikes his father or his mother shall be put to death.
[16]
"Whoever steals a man, whether he sells him or is found in possession of him, shall be put to death.
[17]
"Whoever curses his father or his mother shall be put to death.
[18]
"When men quarrel and one strikes the other with a stone or with his fist and the man does not die but keeps his bed,
[19] then if the man rises again and walks abroad with his staff, he that struck him shall be clear; only he shall pay for the loss of his time, and shall have him thoroughly healed.
[20]
"When a man strikes his slave, male or female, with a rod and the slave dies under his hand, he shall be punished.
[21] But if the slave survives a day or two, he is not to be punished; for the slave is his money.
[22]
"When men strive together, and hurt a woman with child, so that there is a miscarriage, and yet no harm follows, the one who hurt her shall be fined, according as the woman's husband shall lay upon him; and he shall pay as the judges determine.
[23] If any harm follows, then you shall give life for life,
[24] eye for eye, tooth for tooth, hand for hand, foot for foot,
[25] burn for burn, wound for wound, stripe for stripe.
[26]
"When a man strikes the eye of his slave, male or female, and destroys it, he shall let the slave go free for the eye's sake.
[27] If he knocks out the tooth of his slave, male or female, he shall let the slave go free for the tooth's sake.
[28]
"When an ox gores a man or a woman to death, the ox shall be stoned, and its flesh shall not be eaten; but the owner of the ox shall be clear.
[29] But if the ox has been accustomed to gore in the past, and its owner has been warned but has not kept it in, and it kills a man or a woman, the ox shall be stoned, and its owner also shall be put to death.
[30] If a ransom is laid on him, then he shall give for the redemption of his life whatever is laid upon him.

[31] If it gores a man's son or daughter, he shall be dealt with according to this same rule.

[32] If the ox gores a slave, male or female, the owner shall give to their master thirty shekels of silver, and the ox shall be stoned.

[33]

"When a man leaves a pit open, or when a man digs a pit and does not cover it, and an ox or an ass falls into it,

[34] the owner of the pit shall make it good; he shall give money to its owner, and the dead beast shall be his.

[35]

"When one man's ox hurts another's, so that it dies, then they shall sell the live ox and divide the price of it; and the dead beast also they shall divide.

[36] Or if it is known that the ox has been accustomed to gore in the past, and its owner has not kept it in, he shall pay ox for ox, and the dead beast shall be his.

Exod.22

[1]

"If a man steals an ox or a sheep, and kills it or sells it, he shall pay five oxen for an ox, and four sheep for a sheep. He shall make restitution; if he has nothing, then he shall be sold for his theft.

[4] If the stolen beast is found alive in his possession, whether it is an ox or an ass or a sheep, he shall pay double.

[2]

"If a thief is found breaking in, and is struck so that he dies, there shall be no bloodguilt for him;

[3] but if the sun has risen upon him, there shall be bloodguilt for him.

[5]

"When a man causes a field or vineyard to be grazed over, or lets his beast loose and it feeds in another man's field, he shall make restitution from the best in his own field and in his own vineyard.

[6]

"When fire breaks out and catches in thorns so that the stacked grain or the standing grain or the field is consumed, he that kindled the fire shall make full restitution.

[7]

"If a man delivers to his neighbor money or goods to keep, and it is stolen out of the man's house, then, if the thief is found, he shall pay double.

[8] If the thief is not found, the owner of the house shall come near to God, to show whether or not he has put his hand to his neighbor's goods.

[9]

"For every breach of trust, whether it is for ox, for ass, for sheep, for clothing, or for any kind of lost thing, of which one says, 'This is it,' the case of both parties shall come before God; he whom God shall condemn shall pay double to his neighbor.

[10]

"If a man delivers to his neighbor an ass or an ox or a sheep or any beast to keep, and it dies or is hurt or is driven away, without any one seeing it,

[11] an oath by the LORD shall be between them both to see whether he has not put his hand to his neighbor's property; and the owner shall accept the oath, and he shall not make restitution.

[12] But if it is stolen from him, he shall make restitution to its owner.

[13] If it is torn by beasts, let him bring it as evidence; he shall not make restitution for what has been torn.

[14]

"If a man borrows anything of his neighbor, and it is hurt or dies, the owner not being with it, he shall make full restitution.

[15] If the owner was with it, he shall not make restitution; if it was hired, it came for its hire.

[16]

"If a man seduces a virgin who is not betrothed, and lies with her, he shall give the marriage present for her, and make her his wife.

[17] If her father utterly refuses to give her to him, he shall pay money equivalent to the marriage present for virgins.

[18]

"You shall not permit a sorceress to live.

[19]

"Whoever lies with a beast shall be put to death.

[20]

"Whoever sacrifices to any god, save to the LORD only, shall be utterly destroyed.

[21]

"You shall not wrong a stranger or oppress him, for you were strangers in the land of Egypt.

[22] You shall not afflict any widow or orphan.

[23] If you do afflict them, and they cry out to me, I will surely hear their cry;

[24] and my wrath will burn, and I will kill you with the sword, and your wives shall become widows and your children fatherless.

[25]

"If you lend money to any of my people with you who is poor, you shall not be to him as a creditor, and you shall not exact interest from him.

[26] If ever you take your neighbor's garment in pledge, you shall restore it to him before the sun goes down;

[27] for that is his only covering, it is his mantle for his body; in what else shall he sleep? And if he cries to me, I will hear, for I am compassionate.

[28]

"You shall not revile God, nor curse a ruler of your people.

[29]

"You shall not delay to offer from the fulness of your harvest and from the outflow of your presses.

"The first-born of your sons you shall give to me.

[30] You shall do likewise with your oxen and with your sheep: seven days it shall be with its dam; on the eighth day you shall give it to me.

[31]

"You shall be men consecrated to me; therefore you shall not eat any flesh that is torn by beasts in the field; you shall cast it to the dogs.

Exod.23

[1]

"You shall not utter a false report. You shall not join hands with a wicked man, to be a malicious witness.

[2] You shall not follow a multitude to do evil; nor shall you bear witness in a suit, turning aside after a multitude, so as to pervert justice;

[3] nor shall you be partial to a poor man in his suit.

[4]

"If you meet your enemy's ox or his ass going astray, you shall bring it back to him.

[5] If you see the ass of one who hates you lying under its burden, you shall refrain from leaving him with it, you shall help him to lift it up.

[6]

"You shall not pervert the justice due to your poor in his suit.

[7] Keep far from a false charge, and do not slay the innocent and righteous, for I will not acquit the wicked.

[8] And you shall take no bribe, for a bribe blinds the officials, and subverts the cause of those who are in the right.

[9]

"You shall not oppress a stranger; you know the heart of a stranger, for you were strangers in the land of Egypt.

[10]

"For six years you shall sow your land and gather in its yield;

[11] but the seventh year you shall let it rest and lie fallow, that the poor of your people may eat; and what they leave the wild beasts may eat. You shall do likewise with your vineyard, and with your olive orchard.

[12]

"Six days you shall do your work, but on the seventh day you shall rest; that your ox and your ass may have rest, and the son of your bondmaid, and the alien, may be refreshed.

[13] Take heed to all that I have said to you; and make no mention of the names of other gods, nor let such be heard out of your mouth.[2]

[14]

"Three times in the year you shall keep a feast to me.

[15] You shall keep the feast of unleavened bread; as I commanded you, you shall eat unleavened bread for seven days at the appointed time in the month of Abib, for in it you came out of Egypt. None shall appear before me empty-handed.

[16] You shall keep the feast of harvest, of the first fruits of your labor, of what you sow in the field. You shall keep the feast of ingathering at the end of the year, when you gather in from the field the fruit of your labor.

---

[2] As mentioned, following a number of my predecessors (Driver 1911, 241). I see this verse as the closing of the collection of laws. There is some level of repetition of the opening of the collection, where it says, " You need make for me only an altar of earth and sacrifice on it your burnt offerings and your offerings of well-being... in every place where **I cause my name to be** remembered I will come to you and bless you". Compare this to what is written here "Be attentive to all that I have said to you. **Do not invoke the names of other gods**; do not let them be heard on your lips." [Ed. The two verbs use root z. k̲. r̲.] The two texts emphasize the importance of invoking the name of God. In Exodus 23:13 this is an addition to the retrospective of the laws that have been transmitted ("Be attentive to all that I have said to you"). In doing so the verse reveals its role as the closing sentence relative to the opening of the collection of laws. The paragraph in Exodus 23:14-19 is apparently a secondary addition. The commandment to travel to cultic centers during the holidays does not fit well with the folksy ritual philosophy of the northern author who opines the possibility of ritual service anywhere without the need for fancy ritual accessories (Exodus 20: 21-22). Baden (2012, 117) etc., presents another opinion. They also attribute Exodus 23: 14-19, to document E. I believe that this attribution does not adhere to the principle of topical continuity and coherence which Baden emphasizes throughout his book.

[17] Three times in the year shall all your males appear before the Lord GOD.

[18] "You shall not offer the blood of my sacrifice with leavened bread, or let the fat of my feast remain until the morning.

[19] "The first of the first fruits of your ground you shall bring into the house of the LORD your God.

"You shall not boil a kid in its mother's milk.

[20] "Behold, I send an angel before you, to guard you on the way and to bring you to the place which I have prepared.

[21] Give heed to him and hearken to his voice, do not rebel against him, for he will not pardon your transgression; for my name is in him.

[22] "But if you hearken attentively to his voice and do all that I say, then I will be an enemy to your enemies and an adversary to your adversaries.

[23] "When my angel goes before you, and brings you in to the Amorites, and the Hittites, and the Per'izzites, and the Canaanites, the Hivites, and the Jeb'usites, and I blot them out,

[24] you shall not bow down to their gods, nor serve them, nor do according to their works, but you shall utterly overthrow them and break their pillars in pieces.

[25] You shall serve the LORD your God, and I will bless your bread and your water; and I will take sickness away from the midst of you.

[26] None shall cast her young or be barren in your land; I will fulfil the number of your days.

[27] I will send my terror before you, and will throw into confusion all the people against whom you shall come, and I will make all your enemies turn their backs to you.

[28] And I will send hornets before you, which shall drive out Hivite, Canaanite, and Hittite from before you.

[29] I will not drive them out from before you in one year, lest the land become desolate and the wild beasts multiply against you.

[30] Little by little I will drive them out from before you, until you are increased and possess the land.

[**31**] And I will set your bounds from the Red Sea to the sea of the Philistines, and from the wilderness to the Euphra'tes; for I will deliver the inhabitants of the land into your hand, and you shall drive them out before you.

[**32**] You shall make no covenant with them or with their gods.

[**33**] They shall not dwell in your land, lest they make you sin against me; for if you serve their gods, it will surely be a snare to you."

Exod.24

[**3**]³

Moses came and told the people all the words of the LORD and all the ordinances; and all the people answered with one voice, and said, "All the words which the LORD has spoken we will do."

[**4**] And Moses wrote all the words of the LORD. And he rose early in the morning, and built an altar at the foot of the mountain, and twelve pillars, according to the twelve tribes of Israel.

[**5**] And he sent young men of the people of Israel, who offered burnt offerings and sacrificed peace offerings of oxen to the LORD.

[**6**] And Moses took half of the blood and put it in basins, and half of the blood he threw against the altar.

[**7**] Then he took the book of the covenant, and read it in the hearing of the people; and they said, "All that the LORD has spoken we will do, and we will be obedient."

[**8**] And Moses took the blood and threw it upon the people, and said, "Behold the blood of the covenant which the LORD has made with you in accordance with all these words."⁴

[**12**]

The LORD said to Moses, "Come up to me on the mountain, and wait there; and I will give you the tables of stone, with the law and the commandment, which I have written for their instruction."

[**13**] So Moses rose with his servant Joshua, and Moses went up into the mountain of God.

---

³ The author of Exodus 24:1-2 gives Aharon and his sons special status. In doing so he returns to Exodus 19:24 which also marks Aharon's special status. It belongs, apparently to document J (Propp, **Exodus**, B, 145), and therefore I believe that one must also attribute Exodus 24:1-2 to this document as well as their continuation in verses 9-11 (as is the opinion of the commentaries by Dillman, 180; Bacon (1894); Driver (1911), Hyatt (1971), as well as Bacon (1894, 127–131, 132).

⁴ See the previous footnote re: Exodus 24:9-11.

[14] And he said to the elders, "Tarry here for us, until we come to you again; and, behold, Aaron and Hur are with you; whoever has a cause, let him go to them."

[15]

Then Moses went up on the mountain, and the cloud covered the mountain.[5]

[18]

THE GOLDEN CALF

31:18

And he gave to Moses, when he had made an end of speaking with him upon Mount Sinai, the two tables of the testimony,[6] tables of stone, written with the finger of God.

Exod.32

[1]

When the people saw that Moses delayed to come down from the mountain, the people gathered themselves together to Aaron, and said to him, "Up, make us gods, who shall go before us; as for this Moses, the man who brought us up out of the land of Egypt, we do not know what has become of him."

[2] And Aaron said to them, "Take off the rings of gold which are in the ears of your wives, your sons, and your daughters, and bring them to me."

[3] So all the people took off the rings of gold which were in their ears, and brought them to Aaron.

[4] And he received the gold at their hand, and fashioned it with a graving tool, and made a molten calf; and they said, "These are your gods, O Israel, who brought you up out of the land of Egypt!"

[5] When Aaron saw this, he built an altar before it; and Aaron made proclamation and said, "Tomorrow shall be a feast to the LORD."

[6] And they rose up early on the morrow, and offered burnt offerings and brought peace offerings; and the people sat down to eat and drink, and rose up to play.

[7]

---

[5] It is customary to attribute verses Exodus 24: 16-18 to the priestly source. The instructions on how to build the Tabernacle and their appendices in Exodus 25:1-31:17 also stem from this source. See Knohl (1995, 63–68).

[6] The phrase "tablets of the covenant" was coined by priestly editors from the holiness school. They connected the "tablets" from the non-priestly tradition to the "testimony, pact" in the priestly tradition. See my work: Knohl (1995, 67, footnote 21).

And the LORD said to Moses, "Go down; for your people, whom you brought up out of the land of Egypt, have corrupted themselves;

[8] they have turned aside quickly out of the way which I commanded them; they have made for themselves a molten calf, and have worshiped it and sacrificed to it, and said, 'These are your gods, O Israel, who brought you up out of the land of Egypt!'"

[9] And the LORD said to Moses, "I have seen this people, and behold, it is a stiff-necked people;

[10] now therefore let me alone, that my wrath may burn hot against them and I may consume them; but of you I will make a great nation."

[11]

But Moses besought the LORD his God, and said, "O LORD, why does thy wrath burn hot against thy people, whom thou hast brought forth out of the land of Egypt with great power and with a mighty hand?

[12] Why should the Egyptians say, 'With evil intent did he bring them forth, to slay them in the mountains, and to consume them from the face of the earth'? Turn from thy fierce wrath, and repent of this evil against thy people.

[13] Remember Abraham, Isaac, and Israel, thy servants, to whom thou didst swear by thine own self, and didst say to them, 'I will multiply your descendants as the stars of heaven, and all this land that I have promised I will give to your descendants, and they shall inherit it for ever.'"

[14] And the LORD repented of the evil which he thought to do to his people.

[15]

And Moses turned, and went down from the mountain with the two tables of the testimony in his hands, tables that were written on both sides; on the one side and on the other were they written.

[16] And the tables were the work of God, and the writing was the writing of God, graven upon the tables.

[17] When Joshua heard the noise of the people as they shouted, he said to Moses, "There is a noise of war in the camp."

[18] But he said, "It is not the sound of shouting for victory, or the sound of the cry of defeat, but the sound of singing that I hear."

[19] And as soon as he came near the camp and saw the calf and the dancing, Moses' anger burned hot, and he threw the tables out of his hands and broke them at the foot of the mountain.

[20] And he took the calf which they had made, and burnt it with fire, and ground it to powder, and scattered it upon the water, and made the people of Israel drink it.

[21]

And Moses said to Aaron, "What did this people do to you that you have brought a great sin upon them?"

[22] And Aaron said, "Let not the anger of my lord burn hot; you know the people, that they are set on evil.

[23] For they said to me, 'Make us gods, who shall go before us; as for this Moses, the man who brought us up out of the land of Egypt, we do not know what has become of him.'

[24] And I said to them, 'Let any who have gold take it off'; so they gave it to me, and I threw it into the fire, and there came out this calf."

[25]

And when Moses saw that the people had broken loose for Aaron had let them break loose, to their shame among their enemies.

[35]

And the LORD sent a plague upon the people, because they made the calf which Aaron made.[7]

THE OUTER TENT
Exod.33
[7][8]

---

[7] The section of Exodus 32:26-34 contradicts the primary strata of the story of the Golden calf in two ways: according to the primary strata the whole nation sinned with the Golden Calf (Exodus 32:7-8, 20-25, 35), while according to this section the number of sinners was only 3000 people (Exodus 32:8). Likewise, according to the primary strata the sinning nation was punished with a plague (Exodus 32:5), while according to this section they were punished by the Levites' swords (Exodus 26-28). So it seems that this section stems from a different source, J (the text in verse 33 regarding the angel walking among the people as a punishment fits also the J story in Exodus 33:1-6, 12-23). J also used here the ancient poetic description (Deut. 33:9-1) discussed above. Apparently after the destruction of Samaria this northern tradition reached the hands of the author of J. However, as mentioned, he changed the original characteristics of the poetic description. The poem of Deut. 33:8-11 referred to the disagreement that broke out among the tribe of Levi at the waters of Meribah, without any connection to the worship of the calf. However, J copied the location of the events to Mt. Sinai and connected it to the sin of the Golden calf. Likewise, he turned the original conflict story which dealt only with the inner struggle among sons of Levi into a conflict between the tribe of Levi, which did not sin with the Golden Calf at all, and the sinners from other tribes.

[8] I have only referred to Exodus 33:7-11 here in which E describes the establishment of the non-priestly tent of the meeting, the prophetic tent (see Chap. 10, above). As mentioned, the attribution of the verses at the beginning of chapter 34 is complicated and complex and so I have not discussed it here.

Now Moses used to take the tent and pitch it outside the camp, far off from the camp; and he called it the tent of meeting. And every one who sought the LORD would go out to the tent of meeting, which was outside the camp.

[8] Whenever Moses went out to the tent, all the people rose up, and every man stood at his tent door, and looked after Moses, until he had gone into the tent.

[9] When Moses entered the tent, the pillar of cloud would descend and stand at the door of the tent, and the LORD would speak with Moses.

[10] And when all the people saw the pillar of cloud standing at the door of the tent, all the people would rise up and worship, every man at his tent door.

[11] Thus the LORD used to speak to Moses face to face, as a man speaks to his friend. When Moses turned again into the camp, his servant Joshua the son of Nun, a young man, did not depart from the tent.

BIBLIOGRAPHY

M. Aberbach and L. Smolar, 1967, "Aaron, Jeroboam and the Golden Calves", *JBL* 86, 129–140.

S. Abramsky, 1954, "The Qenites", *EI* 3 (1954), 116–124 [in Hebrew].

Y. Aharoni, 1974, "The Horned Altar of Beer-sheba", *BA* 37, 2–6.

S. Ahituv, 1995, *Joshua* (Mikra Leyisrael), Tel Aviv 1995 [in Hebrew].

S. Ahituv, *HaKetav VeHaMiktav Handbook of Ancient Inscriptions from the Land of Israel and the Kingdoms beyond the Jordan*[2], Jerusalem [In Hebrew].

S. Ahituv, "Moses", *EB*, vol. V, col. 482–496 [in Hebrew].

S. Ahituv, "Tubal-Qain", *EB*, vol. VIII, col. 462 [in Hebrew].

R. Albertz, 2018, "The Recent Discussion on the Formation of the Pentateuch/Hexateuch", *Hebrew Studies* 59, 65–92.

A. Alt, "The Origins of the Israelite Law" (1934), in: *Essays on Old Testament History and Religion* (Eng. Transl.: R.A. Wilson), Garden City NY 1967, 101–171.

N. Amzalleg, 2009, "Yahweh, the Canaanite God of Metallurgy?", *JSOT* 33, 387–404.

N. Amzallag, 2014, "Some Implications of the Vulcanic Theophany of YHWH on His Primeval Identity", *Antiguo Oriente* 12, 11–38.

N. Amzallag, 2015, "The Origin and Evolution of the Saraph Symbol", *Antiguo Oriente* 13, 99–126.

F.I. Andersen, 2001, *Habakkuk* (AB), New York NY.

H. Ausloos, 2013, "The 'Proto-Deuteronomist': Fifty Years Later", *OTE* 26, 531–558.

I. Knohl, *Biblical Sinai traditions*,
https://doi.org/10.1007/978-3-031-77983-1

U. Avner, 2014, "Egyptian Timna — Reconsiderd", in: J.M. Tebes (ed.), *Unearthing the Wilderness: Studies on the History and Archaeology of the Negev and Edom in the Iron Age* (Ancient Near Eastern Studies Supp. 45), Leuven-Paris-Walpole MA, 103–162.

B.W. Bacon, 1894, *The Triple Tradition of the Exodus*, Hartford.

J.S. Baden, 2012, *The Composition of the Pentateuch: Renewing the Documentary Hypothesis*, New Haven.

א' ברטל, "עלייתה ושקיעתה של תנועת בני הנביאים בימי אליהו ואלישע", ספר יעקב Bartal, 1979, גיל, ירושלים, 41–63.

J. Begrich, 1935, "Die priestliche Torah", in P. Volz et al. (eds.), *Werden und Wesen des Alten Testaments* (BZAW 66), Berlin, 63–88.

J. Blenkinsopp, 1999, "Deuteronomic Contribution to the Narrative in Genesis — Numbers: A Test Case", in: L.S. Schearing and S. L. McKenzie (eds.), *Those Elusive Deuteronomists: The Phenomenon of 'Pandeuteronomism'* (JSOTSup. 268), Sheffield, 84–115.

J. Blenkinsopp, 2008, "The Midianite-Kenite Hypothesis Revisited and the Origins of Judah", *JSOT* 33, 131–153.

Y. Bloch and N. Wasserman, 2021, "Blood Guilt and Monetary Compensation in Biblical Laws and Mari Letters", *Beit Mikra* 66, 7–32 [in Hebrew].

E. Blum, 2012, "Der historische Mose und die Frühgeschichte Israels", *HeBai* 1, 37–63.

T. Booij, 1984a, "Mountain and Theophany in the Sinai Narrative", *Biblica* 65, 1–26.

T. Booij, 1984b, "The Background of the Oracle in Psalm 81", *Biblica* 65, 465–475.

C. Brekelmans, 1966, "Die sogenanten deuteronomistischen Elemente in Gen. bis Num.: Ein Beitrag zur Vorgeschichte des Deuteronomiums", *SVT* 15, 90–96.

M. Broshi, 1974, "The Expansion of Jerusalem in the Reigns of Hezekiah and Manasseh", *IEJ* 24, 21–26.

K. Budde, 1897, *Das Buch der Richter* (KHC), Freiburg-Leipzig-Tübingen.

A. Burlingame, 2019, "Writing and Literacy in the World of Ancient Israel: Recent Developments and Future Directions", *Bibliotheca Orientalis* 76, 46–74.

A.F. Campbell, 1986, *Of Prophets and Kings: A Late Ninth-Century Document (1 Samuel 1-2 Kings 10)* (CBQMS 17), Washington DC.

U.M.D. Cassuto, "Deuteronomy Chapter xxxiii and the New Year in Ancient Israel", in: idem, *Biblical and Oriental Studies* (Engl. transl. by I. Abrahams), vol. I–II, Jerusalem 1975, vol. I, 47–70 (1928).

U.M.D. Cassuto, "The Israelite Epic", in idem, Biblical and Oriental Studies, vol. II, 69–112.

S. Chavel, 2015, "A Kingdom of Priests and its Earthen Altars in Exodus 19-24", *VT* 65, 169–222.

B.S. Childs, 1974, *Exodus* (OTL), London.

Y.H. Chung, 2010, *The Sin of the Calf: The Rise of the Bible's Negative Attitude Toward the Golden Calf*, London — New York.

כדורי, תשע"א' אי" כדורי, "שירת המקרא — הא כיצד?", בתוך: ע' טלשיר (עורכת), ספרות המקרא: 287 א', ירושלים, מחקרים, ומבואות –306. ; Ya'akov Kaduri (James L. Kugel) –"Biblical Poetry", in: Z. Talshir (ed.) *Literature of the Hebrew Bible: introductions and studies, Jerusalem* 2011, 287–286.

C. Cohen, 1969, "Was the P Document Secret?", *JANES* 112, 39–44.

F.M. Cross, 1973, *Canaanite Myth and Hebrew Epic*, Cambridge MA.

J.C. Darnell, F.W. Dobbs-Allsopp, M.J. Lundberg, P.K. McCarter, B. Zuckerman and C. Manassa, 2005, "Two Early Alphabetic Inscriptions from the Wadi el-Ḥôl: New Evidence for the Origin of the Alphabet from the Western Desert of Egypt", *AASOR* 59, 64–124.

S. Dalley, 1990, "Yahweh in Hamath in the 8th Century BC: Cuneiform Material and Historical Deductions", *VT* 40, 21–32.

P.R. Davies, 2007, "The Trouble with Benjamin", in: R. Rezetko et al. (eds.), *Reflection and Refraction (Fs. A.G. Auld)* (SVT 113), Leiden, 93–111.

D. DeJong, 2022, *A Prophet like Moses (Deut 18:15, 18) The Origin, History, and Influence of the Mosaic Prophetic Succession* (SJSJ 205), Leiden and Boston.

A. Dillmann, 1886, *Die Bücher Numeri, Deuteronomium und Josua2* (KEHAT), Leipzig.

A. Dillmann, 1890, *Die Bücher Exodus und Leviticus* (KEHAT), Leipzig.

S.R. Driver, 1902, *Deuteronomy* (ICC) (2nd ed.), Edinburgh.

S.R. Driver, 1911, *Exodus* (CB), Cambridge.

J.E. Dunn, 2014, "A God of Volcanoes: Did Yahwism Take Root in Volcanic Ashes?", *JSOT* 38, 387–424.

C. Echols, 2008, *"Tell Me O Muse": The Song of Deborah (Judges 5) in the Light of Heroic Poetry*, New York-London.

Carl S. Ehrlich, 2012, "'Noughty' Moses: A Decade of Moses Scholarship 2000-2010", *HeBaI* 1, 93–110.

R. Eichler, 2011, "The Function of the Ark Cherubim", *Tarbiz* 79, 165–185 [in Hebrew].

R. Eichler, 2014, "The Meaning of הַכְּרֻבִים יֹשֵׁב", *ZAW* 126, 358–371.

N.N. El-Masry et al., 2013, "Historical Accounts of the AD 1256 Eruption near Al-Madina", *Vorisa Scientific Meeting (November 17–18 2013) Conference Paper*, 9–13.

Y. Elitzur, 2012, *Ancient Toponyms in the Land of Israel: Preservation and History* (2nd ed.), Jerusalem [in Hebrew].

J.A. Emerton, 2006, "The Kingdoms of Judah and Israel and Ancient Hebrew History Writing", in: S.E. Fassberg and H. Hurvitz (eds.), *Biblical Hebrew in the Northwest Semitic Setting*, Jerusalem – Winona Lake IN, 33–49.

Z. Farber, 2016, *Images of Joshua in the Bible and its reception* (BZAW 457), Berlin.

A. Faust, 2013, "Early Israel: An Egalitarian Society", *BAR* 39/4, 45–49.

Y. Feder, 2010, "A Levantine Tradition: The Kizzuwatnean Blood Rite and Biblical Sin Offering", in: Y. Cohen et al. (eds.), *Pax Hethitica (Fs. I. Zinger)*, Wiesbaden, 101–114.

Y. Feder, 2011, *Blood Expiation in Hittite and Biblical Ritual: Origigns, Context and Meaning*, Atlanta GA.

Y. Feder, 2013, "The Aniconic Tradition, Deuteronomy 4 and the Politics of Israelite Identity", *JBL* 132, 251–274.

J.P. Fokkelman, *Major Poems of the Hebrew Bible*, I-IV, Assen 1998–2004.

D. Fleming, 2020, *Yahweh before Israel*, Cambridge.

Israel Finkelstein, 2008, "The Settlement History of Jerusalem in the Eighth and Seventh Centuries BC", *RB* 115, 499–515.

I. Finkelstein, 2013, *The Forgotten Kingdom: The Archaeology and History of Northern Israel*, Atlanta GA.

Israel Finkelstein, 2020, "The Emergence and Dissemination of Writing in Judah", *Semitica et Classica* 13, 269–282.

I. Finkelstein and B. Sass, 2013, "Alphabetic Inscriptions, Late Bronze II to Iron IIA: Archeological Context , Distribution and Chronology", *HeBaI* 2, 149–220.

I. Finkelstein and N.A. Silberman, 2001, *The Bible Unearthed: Archaeology's New Vision of Ancient Israel and the Origin of Its Sacred Texts*, New York.

I. Finkelstein and N.A. Silberman, 2006, *David and Solomon: In Search of the Bible's Sacred Kings and the Roots of the Western Tradition*, New York.

Joel J. Finkelstein, 1963, "Mesopotamian Historiography", *Proceedings of the American Philosophical Society* 107, 461–472.

M. Fishbane, 1980, "Biblical Colophons, Textual Criticism and Legal Analogies", *CBQ* 42, 438–449.

David N. Freedman, 1980, "The Poetic Structure of the Framework of Deuteronomy 33", in: G.A. Rendsburg et al. (eds.), *The Bible World (Fs. Cyrus H. Gordon)*, New York, 25–46.

S. Freud, *Der Mann Moses und die monotheistische Religion*, Amsterdam 1939.

C. Frevel, 2021, "When and from Where did YHWH Emerge? Some Reflections on Early Yahwism in Israel and Judah", *Entangled Religions* 12.2: *The Desert Origins of God: Yahweh's Emergence and Early History in the Southern Levant and Northern Arabia* (32pp.).

Richard E. Friedman, 1981, "From Egypt to Egypt: Dtr1 and Dtr2", in: B. Halpern and J.D. Levenson (ed.), *Traditions in Transformation: Turning Points in Biblical Faith*, Winona Lake IN, 167–192.

R.E. Friedman, "Torah (Pentateuch)", *ABD*, VI, New York 1992, 609–633.

S. Ganor and I. Kreimerman, 2017, "An Eighth Century B.C.E. Gate Shrine at Tel Lachish, Israel", *BASOR* 381, 211–236.

B.T. German, 2013, "Moses at Marah", *VT* 63, 47–58.

H. Gese, 1964, "Der Davidsbund und die Zionserwählung", *ZTK* 61, 10–26.

H.L. Ginsberg, 1982, *The Israelian Heritage of Judaism*, New York.

R.K. Gnuse, 2000, "Redefining the Elohist", *JBL* 119, 201–220.

D. Goitein, 1956, "YHWH the Passionate: The Monotheistic Meaning and Origin of the Name YHWH", *VT* 6, 1–9.

J. Goldingay, *Psalms* (Baker Commentary on the Old Testament Wisdom and Psalms), I-III, Ada MI 2006–2008.

O. Goldwasser, 2006, "King Apophis of Avaris and the Emergence of Monotheism", in: E. Czerny et al. (eds.), *Timelines: Studies in Honour of Manfred Bietak* (Orientalia Lovaniensia Analecta 149), I-III, Leuven, II, 129–133.

O. Goldwasser, 2015, "The Invention of the Alphabet: On 'Lost Papyri' and the Egyptian Alphabet", in: C. Rico and C. Attucci (eds.), *Origins of the Alphabet: Proceedings of the First Polis Institute Interdisciplinary Conference*, Cambridge, 124–140.

O. Goldwasser, 2022, "The Early Alphabetic Inscriptions Found by the Shrine of Hathor at Serabit el-Khadem: Palaeography, Materiality, and Agency", *IEJ* 72, 14–48.

M. Greenberg, 1960, "נסה in Exodus 20 20 and the Porpuse of the Sinaitic Theophany", *JBL* 79, 273–276.

M. Greenberg, 1961, "Some Postulates of Biblical Criminal Law", in: M. Haran (ed.), *Yehezkel Kaufmann Jubilee Volume*, Jerusalem, 5–28.

H. Gressmann, 1913, *Mose und seine Zeit: Ein Kommentar zu den Mose-Sagen*, Göttingen.

J.G. Griffiths, 1953, "The Egyptian Derivation of the Name Moses", *JNES* 12, 225–231.

K. Gross, 1931, "Hoseas Einfluss auf Jeremias Anschauungen", *NKZ* 42, 241–255, 327–343.

P. Guillaume, 2008, "Jerusalem 720-705 BCE. No Flood of Israelite Refugees", *SJOT* 22, 195–211.

H. Gunkel, *Die Psalmen* (GHAT), Göttingen 1926, (6th repr. 1986).

B. Halpern, 2000, "The State of Israelite History", in: G.N. Knoppers and J.G. McConville (eds.), *Reconsidering Israel and Judah*, Winona Lake IN, 540–565.

M. Haran, 1956, "The Tent of Meeting", *Tarbiz* 25, 11–20 [in Hebrew].

M. Haran, 1962, "Shiloh and Jerusalem: The Origin of the Priestly Tradition in the Pentateuch", *JBL* 81, 14–24.

M. Haran, 1973, מ' הרן, תקופות ומוסדות במקרא: עיונים היסטוריים, תל אביב, *Ages and institutions in the Bible*, Tel Aviv.

M. Haran, 1981, "Behind the Scenes of History: Determining the Date of the Priestly Source", *JBL* 100, 321–333.

Z. Herzog, 2010, "Perspectives on Southern Israel's Cult Centralization: Arad and Beer-Sheba", in: R. G. Kratz and H. Spieckermann (eds.), *One God—One*

Cult—One Nation: Archaeological and Biblical Perspectives (BZAW 405), Berlin, 169–199.

Y. Hoffman, 1982, "Exigencies of Genre in Deuteronomy", *Shnaton* 5–6, 41–54 [in Hebrew].

R.D. Holmstedt, 2014, "Analyzing זֶה Grammar and Reading זֶהTexts of Ps 68:9 and Judg 5:5", *JHS* 14, 27pp.

F.L. Hossfeld — E. Zenger, *Psalms* (Engl. Ttansl. by L.M. Maloney) (Hermeneia), I-III, Minneapolis 2005–2011.

A.V. Hurowitz, 1983, "The Golden Calf and the Tabernacle", *Shnaton* 7–8, 51–59 [in Hebrew].

A.V. Hurowitz, 2012, *Proverbs* ((Mikra Leyisrael), vol. I–II, Tel Aviv [in Hebrew].

J.P. Hyatt, 1971, *Exodus* (NCBC), London.

D.W. Jamieson-Drake, 1991, *Scribes and Schools in Monarchic Judah: A Socio-Archaeological Approach*, Sheffield.

A. Jenks, 1977, *The Elohist and the North Israelite Traditions* (SBLMS 22), Missoula MT.

D. Jericke, "Meribath-kadesh", *EBR*, 18, 760–761.

S. Jiang, 2022, "How Prophecy Critiquing Socio-Economic Injustice Transformed into Law: The Cases of the Covenant Code and Early Prophetic Texts", *ZAW* 134, 441–457.

I. Kalimi, 1988, "Three Assumptions About the Kenites", *ZAW* 100, 386–393.

I. Kalimi, 2005, *The Reshaping of Ancient Israelite History in Chronicles*, Winona Lake IN.

R. S. Kawashima, 2004, *Biblical Narrative and the Death of the Rhapsode*, Bloomington IN.

S. Kleiman, A. Kleiman and E. Ben-Yosef, 2017, "Metalworers' Material Culture in the Early Iron Age Levant: The Ceramic Assemblage from Site 34 (Slave's Hill) in the Timna Valley", *Tel Aviv* 44, 232–264.

E.A. Knauf, *Midian*, Wiesbaden, 1988.

E.A. Knauf, 2002, "Towards an Archaeology of the Hexateuch", in: J.C. Gertz et al. (eds.), *Abschied vom Jahwisten* (BZAW 315), Berlin, 277–294.

E.A. Knauf, 2006, "Bethel: The Israelite Impact on Judean Language and Literature", in: O. Lipschits and M. Oeming (ed.), *Judah and the Judeans in the Persian Period*, Winona Lake IN, 291–350.

I. Knohl, 1995, *The Sanctuary of Silence: The Priestly Torah and the Holiness School*, Minneapolis.

I. Knohl, 1997, "Two Aspects of the 'Tent of Meeting'", in: M. Cogan et al. (eds.), *Tehila le-Moshe (Fs. M. Greenberg)*, Winona Lake IN, 73–78.

I. Knohl, 2003, *The Divine Symphony: The Bible's Many Voices*, Philadelphia PA.

I. Knohl, 2012a, "Sacred Architecture: The Numerical Dimensions of Biblical Poetry", *VT* 62, 189–197.

I. Knohl, 2012b, "God's Victory over 'the Olden Gods': Theological Corrections in Deuteronomy 33.12,27", in: F.H. Polak and A. Brenner (eds.), *Words, Ideas, Worlds; Biblical Essays in Honour of Yairah Amit*, Sheffield, 145–149.

I. Knohl, 2012c, "Psalm 68: Structure, Composition and Geography", *JHS* 12, 22pp.

I. Knohl, 2015, "P and Traditions of Northern Syria and Southern Anatolia", in: F. Landy et al. (eds.), *Text, Time and Temple: Historical and Ritual Studies in Leviticus*, Sheffield, 63–69.

I. Knohl, 2019, *The Messiah Controversy: Who Are the Jews Waiting For?*, Tel Aviv [in Hebrew].

I. Knohl, 2023a, (Recension:[S. Ahituv, *Hosea* (Mikra Leyisrael), Tel Aviv 2022]), *Beit Mikra* 68, 177–182.

I. Knohl, 2023b, "THE SONG OF DEBORAH: HUMAN HEROISM OR DIVINE SALVATION", *Reshit: Studies in Judaism* 7, 1–22.

O. Komlós, 1956, "תכו לרגלך(Deut. XXXIII 3)", *VT* 6, 435–436.

H.J. Kraus, *Psalms* (Engl. Transl. by H.O. Oswald), I-II, Minneapolis 1988–1989.

J. L. Kugel, 2011, "Biblical Poetry", in: Z. Talshir et al. (eds.) *The Literature of the Hebrew Bible*, Yad Ben-Zvi Press, Jerusalem, 3–36.

S.C. Layton, 1988, "Jehoseph n Ps 81,6", *Biblica* 69, 406–411.

A. Lemaire, 1990, "Joas, roi d'Israël, et la première rédaction du cycle d'Élisée", in:C. Brekelmans and J. Lust (eds.), *Pentateuchal and Deuteronomistic Studies; Papers Read at the XIIIth IOSOT Congress, Leuven, 1989*, Leuven, 245–254.

A. Lemaire, 1991, "Géhazi et les "hauts faits d'Élisée" : remarques sur l'histoire de la rédaction des cycles d'Élie et d'Élisée", in: J.J. Adler (ed.), *Haim M.I. Gevaryahu Memorial Volume*, I-II, Jerusalem, II, 41–52.

M. Leunenberger, 2010, "Jhwhs Herkunft aus dem Süden. Archäologische Befunde-biblische Überlieferungen — historische Korrelationen", *ZAW* 122, 1–19.

M. Leunenberger, 2017, "YHWH's Provenance from the South: A New Evaluation of the Arguments pro and contra", in: J. van Oorschot and M. Witte (eds.), The Origins of Yahwism (BZAW 484), Berlin-Boston, 157–179.

B.M. Levinson, 1997, *Deuteronomy and the Hermeneutics of Legal Innovation*, Oxford.

T.J. Lewis, *The Origin and Character of God: Ancient Israelite Religion through the Lens of Divinity*, Oxford 2020.

S.A. Loewenstamm, "Jethro", *EB*, vol. III, 954–957.

S.A. Loewenstamm, 1958, "The Bearing of Psalm 81 upon the Problem of Exodus", *EI* 5, 80–82.

ש"א ליונשטם, "רעדת הטבע בשעת הופעת ה'", "עז לדוד", Loewenstamm, 1964, ירושלים, 520–508.

S.A. Loewenstamm, 1971, "The Investiture of Levi" (1971), in: idem, From Babylon to Canaan: Studies in the Bible and Its Oriental Background (ed. By Y. Avishur and J. Blau), Jerusalem 1992, 55–65.

M. Luciani, 2016, "Mobility, Contacts and definition of Culture(s) in New Archeological Research in North East Arabia", in M. Luciani (ed.), *The Archeology of North Arabiah*, Vienna, 21–57.

M. Luciani, 2018, "Pottery from the "Midianite Heartland"? On Tell Kheleifeh and Qurayyah Painted Ware. New Evidence from the Harvard Semitic Museum", in: L. Nehmé & A. Al-Jallad, *To the Madbar and Back Again (Fs. M.C.A Macdonald)*, Leiden, 392–438.

N. MacDonald, 2012, "Anticipation of Horeb: Exodus 17 as Inner-Biblical Commentary", in: G. Khan and D. Lipton (eds.), *Studies on the Text and Versions of the Hebrew Bible in Honour of Robert Gordon*, Leiden, 7–20.

A. Malamat, 1962, "Mari and the Bible: Some Patterns of Tribal Organization and Institutions", *JAOS* 82, 143–150.

D. Markel, 2019, "The Redactional Theologization of the Book of the Covenant: A Study in Criteriology", *BN* 181, 47–61.

A.D.H. Mayes, 1979, *Deuteronomy* (NCBC), Grand Rapids MI.

B. Mazar, 1947, "The Scribe of King David and the Problem of the High Officials in the Ancient Kingdom of Israel", *BJPES* 13, 105–114 [in Hebrew].

S.L. Mckenzie, 1991, *The Trouble with Kings: The Composition of the Book of Kings in the Deuteronomistic History* (SVT 42), Leiden.

S.L. Mckenzie, 2019, 1 Kings 16 - 2 Kings 16 (IECOT), Stuttgart.

A. Millard, 2010, "'Take a Large Tablet and Write on it': Isaiah – A Writing Prophet?", in: K.J. Dell et al. (eds.), *Genesis, Isaiah and Psalms (Fs. J.A. Emerton)*, Leiden, 105–117.

R.D. Miller II, 2021, *Yahweh: Origin of a Desert God* (FRLANT 284), Göttingen.

J.C. de Moor, 1990, *The Rise of Yahwism: The Roots of Israelite Monotheism*, Leuven.

Y. Muffs, 1992, *Love & Joy: Law, Language and Religion in Ancient Israel*, New York NY.

M. Münnich, 2005, "The Cult of Bronze Serpents in Ancient Canaan and Israel", *Iggud: Selected Essays in Jewish Studies* 14, vol. 1, 39*–56*.

N. Na'aman, 1996, "The Contribution of the Amarna Letters to the Debate on Jerusalem's Political Position in the Tenth Century B.C.E", *BASOR* 304, 17–27.

N. Na'aman, 2002, *The Past that Shapes the Present. The Creation of Biblical Historiography in the Late First Temple Period and After the Downfall* (Yeriot 3), Jerusalem.

N. Na'aman, 2007, "When and How Did Jerusalem Become a Great City? The Rise of Jerusalem as Judah's Premier City in the Eighth-Seventh Centuries B.C.E.", *BASOR* 347, 21–56.

N. Na'aman, 2009, "Saul, Benjamin and the Emergence of 'Biblical Israel'", *ZAW* 121, 211–224, 335–349.

N. Na'aman, 2014, "Dismissing the Myth of a Flood of Israelite Refugees in the Late Eighth Century BCE", *ZAW* 126, 1–14.

N. Na'aman, 2016, "The 'Kenite Hypothesis' in the Light of the Excavations at Horvat 'Uza", in: G. Bartoloni & M.G. Biga (eds.), *Not Only History*, Winona Lake IN, 171–182.

H. Najman, 2009, *Seconding Sinai*, Atlanta.

E. Nielsen, 1982, "Moses and the Law", *VT* 32, 87–98.

M. Nissinen, 2014, "Since When Do Prophets Write?", in: K. de Troyer et al. (eds.), *In the Footsteps of Sherlock Holmes (Fs. A. Aejmelaus)*, Leuven, 585–606.

M. Noth, *Numbers* (Transl. by J.D. Martin) (OTL), London 1968.

H.T. Obbink, 1929, "Jahwebilder", *ZAW* 47, 264–274.

S. Olyan, 1996, "Why an Altar of Unfinished Stones? Some Thoughts on Ex 20, 25 and Dtn 27, 5-6", *ZAW* 108, 161–171.

Eckart Otto, 1996, "The Pre-exilic Deuteronomy as a Revision of the Covenant Code", in: idem, *Kontinuum und Proprium. Studien zur Sozial- und Rechtsgeschichte des Alten Orients und des Alten Testaments, Orientalia Biblica et Christiana*, Wiesbaden, 112–122.

E. Otto, 2007, *Mose: Geschichte und Legende*, München.

E. Otto, *Deuteronomium* (HThKAT), I-IV, Freiburg-Basel-Wien, 2012–2016.

Susanne Otto, 2003, "The Composition of the Elijah-Elisha Stories and the Deuteronomistic History", *JSOT* 27, 487–508.

H. Pfeiffer, 2005, *Jahwes Kommen von Süden: Jdc 5; Hab 3; Dtn 33 und Ps 68 in ihrem literatur- und theologiegeschichtlicen Umfeld* (FRLANT 211), Göttingen.

O. Procksch, 1906, *Das nordhebräische Sagenbuch: Die Elohimquelle*, Leipzig.

W.H.C. Propp, 1987, *Water in the Wilderness* (HSM 68), Atlanta GA.

W.H.C. Propp, *Exodus* (AB), I-II, New York 1998–2006.

Rabin, 1970, ח' רבין, "מלים בעברית המקראית מלשון האינדו־אריים שבמזרח הקרוב", ש' אברמסקי, ואחרים (עורכים), ספר שמואל ייבין, ירושלים, 462–497.

R. Reich, O. Lernau and E. Shukron, 2007, "Recent Discoveries in the City of David, Jerusalem", *IEJ* 57, 153–169.

M. Richelle, 2016, "Elusive Scrolls: Could Any Hebrew Literature Have Been Written Prior to the Eighth Century BCE?" *VT* 66, 556–594.

Rofé, 1978, א' רופא, "ברכת משה, מקדש נבו ושאלת מוצא הלויים (דב' ל"ג)", בתוך: ספר ש"א ליונשטם, ירושלים 424; נדפס–תשל"ח, 409 שנית אצל הנ"ל, מבוא לספר דברים, ירושלים 249–תשמ"ח, 234.

A. Rofé, 1988a, *The Prophetical Stories: The Narratives About the Prophets in the Hebrew Bible, Their Literary Types and History*, Jerusalem.

A. Rofé, 1988b, "Qumranic Paraphrases, the Greek Deuteronomy and the Late History of the Biblical נשיא", *Textus* 14, 163–174.

A. Rofé, 1988c, "The Vineyard of Naboth: The Origin and Message of the Story", *VT* 38, 89–104.

A. Rofé, 1991, "Ephraimite versus Deuteronomistic history", in: D. Garrone and F. Israel (eds.), *Storia e tradizioni di Israele; scritti in onore di J. Alberto Soggin*, Brecia, 221–235.

A. Rofé, 2004, "Joshua Son of Nun in the History of Biblical Tradition", *Tarbiz* 73, 333–364 [in Hebrew].

A. Rofé, 2009, *Introduction to the Literature of the Hebrew Bible*, Jerusalem.

A. Rofe, 2014, *The Stories of the Prophets*, [Heb.], Jerusalem.

A. Rofé, 2015, "Text and Context: The Textual Elimination of the Names of Gods and its Literary, Administrative, and Legal Context", in: C. Warman (ed.), *From Author to Copyist; Essays on the Composition, Redaction, and Transmission of the Hebrew Bible in Honor of Zipi Talshir*, Winona Lake, IN, 63–79.

M. Roi, 2012, "The Story of Elijah's Flight (1 Kings 19): A Comparative Study on the Pattern of 'Departure Stories' in the Bible", *Shnaton* 21, 69–92 [in Hebrew].

M. Roi, 2020, ""You Shall Worship God on This Mountain" (Exod 3:12) as a Key to Revealing the Roots of the Sinai Covenant", *Beit Mikra* 65, 138–163 [in Hebrew].

C.A. Rollston, 2010, *Writing and Literacy in the World of Ancient Israel: Epigraphic Evidence from the Iron Age*, Atlanta GA.

C.A. Rollston, 2017, "Epigraphic Evidence from Jerusalem and its Environs at the Dawn of Biblical History: Methodologies and a Long Duree Perspective", *NSJAR* XI, 7*–20*.

C.A. Rollston, 2018, "Scripture and Inscriptions: Eighth-Century Israel and Judah in Writing", in: Z.I. Farber and J.L. Wright (eds.), *Archaeology and History of Eighth-Century Judah*, Atlanta GA, 457–473.

D. Rom-Shiloni, 2015, ""On the day I Took Them out of the Land of Egypt": A Non-Deuteronomic Phrase within Jeremiah's Conception of Covenant", *VT* 65, 621–647.

T. Römer, 2013, "Zwischen Urkunden, Fragmenten und Ergänzungen: Zum Stand der Pentateuchforschung", *ZAW* 125, 2–24.

T. Römer, 2015a, *The Invention of God* (Eng. Transl.: R. Geuss), Cambridge MA – London.

T. Römer, 2015b, *Moïse en version originale: Enquête sur le récit de la sortie d'Égypte*.

B. Rothenberg, 1988, *The Egyptian Minings Temple at timna*, London.

B. Rothenberg & J. Glass, 1983, 'The Midianite Pottery', in J.F.A. Sawyer & D.J.A. Clines (eds.) *Midian, Moab and Edom: The History and Archaeology of Late Bronze and Iron Age Jordan and North-West Arabia* (JSOTSup. 24), Sheffield, 65–124.

B. Sass, 1991, "The Beth Shemesh Tablet and the Early History of the Proto-Canaanite, Cuneiform and South Semitic Alphabets", *UF* 23, 315–326.

F. Schipper, 2008, "Kadesch-Barnea", *WiBiLex*, 7pp. https://www.bibelwissen-schaft.de/wibilex/das-bibellexikon/lexikon/sachwort/anzeigen/details/kadesch-barnea/ch/f96d37f9a2e03af1b36258da17dce3e7/   (retrieved 01/01/2023).

K. Schmid, 2010, *Genesis and the Moses Story: Israel's Dual Origins in the Hebrew Bible* (Eng. Transl. by J.D. Nogalski), Winona Lake IN.

K. Schmid, 2012, *The Old Testament: A Literary History* (eng. transl.: L.M. Malony), Minneapolis.

S. Schneider, 2019, "Moses in Cush", *Jewis Bible Quarterly*, 47, 113–119.

W.M. Schniedewind, 2004, *How the Bible Became a Book: The Textualization of Ancient Israel*, Cambridge.

B. J. Schwartz, "What Really Happened at Mount Sinai?", *BR* (October 1997), 21–46.

B.J. Schwartz, 2009, "The Visit of Jethro: A Case of Chronological Displacement? The Source-Critical Solution", in: N.S. Fox et al. (eds.), *Mishneh Todah: Studies in Deuteronomy and Its Cultural Environment in Honor of Jeffery H. Tigay*, Winona Lake IN, 29–48.

B.J. Schwartz, 2021, "The Documentary Hypothesis", in: J.S. Baden and J. Stackert (eds.), *The Oxford Handbook of the Pentateuch*, Oxford, 165–187.

I.L. Seeligmann, 1964, "A Psalm from Pre-Regal Times", *VT* 14, 75–92.

M. Seidel, "Parallels between Isaiah and Psalms", in: idem, *Chiqre Miqra*, Jerusalem 1978, 1–97 [in Hebrew].

Theodor Seidl, 1993, "Mose und Elija am Gottesberg: Überlieferungen zu Krise und Konversion der Propheten", *BZ* 37, 1–25.

Seri Levi, 2020, א' סרי-לוי, הכעס האלוהי והדרכים לשיכוכו בתורה ובמקורותיה (דיסרטציה), ירושלים. A. Seri – Levi, Divine Anger and its Appeasement, Dissertation, The Hebrew University.

A. Seri-Levi, 2023, "The Yahawistic Account of the Theophany at Sinai. The Establishment of the Divine Presence", in: J.S. Baden and J. Stackert (eds.), *The Pentateuch and Its Readers* (Fs. B.J. Schwartz) (FAT 170), Tübingen, 53–82.

R. Shlomi Hen, 2021, "Signs of YHWH, God of the Hebrews, in New Kingdom Egypt?", *Entangled Religions* 12, 16pp.

I. Singer, "The Hittites and the Bible Revisited", in: A.M. Maeir and P. de Miroschedji (eds.), *"I Will Speak Riddles of Ancient Times" (Fs. Amihai Mazar)*, I-II, Winona Lake IN 2006, I, 723–756.

B.D. Sommer, 2015, *Revelation and Authority: Sinai in Jewish Scripture and Tradition* (The Anchor Yale Bible Reference Library), New Haven CT.

Morton Smith, 1971, "Pseudoepigraphy in the Israelite Tradition" (1971), repr. in S.J.D. Cohen (ed.), *Studies in the Cult of Yahwe*, I-II, Leiden 1995–1996, I, 55–72.

J. Stackert, 2014, *A Prophet Like Moses: Prophecy, Law, and Israelite Religion*, Oxford.

C. Steuernagel, 1912, *Einleitung in das Alte Testament*, Tübingen.

C. Steuernagel, 1923, *Die Bücher Deuteronomium und Josua* 2 (GHAT), Göttingen.

M.E. Tate, *Psalms* (WBC), vol. I–II, Grand Rapids MI 1990–1991.

S.L. Terrien, 2003, The Psalms: Strophic Structure and Theological Commentary, Grand Rapids MI.

J.H. Tigay, 2004, "The Presence of God and the Coherence of Exodus 20:22-26", in: C. Cohen et al. (eds.), *Sefer Moshe: The Moshe Weinfeld Jubilee Volume*, Winona Lake IN, 195–211.

J.H. Tigay, 2016, Deuteronomy (Mikra Leyisrael), vol. I–II, Tel Aviv.

A. Toeg, 1969, "A Textual Note on 1 Samuel XIV 41", *VT* 19, 493–498.

A. Toeg, 1977, *Lawgiving at Sinai*, Jerusalem [in Hebrew].

K. van der Toorn, 2007, *Scribal Culture and the Making of the Hebrew Bible*, Cambridge MA – London.

K. van der Toorn, "Yahweh", *Dictionary of Deities and Demons in the Bible*2, (ed. by K. van der Toorn et al.), Leiden 1999, 910–919.

B. Uffenheimer, 2001, *Classical Prophecy: The Prophetic Consciousness*, Jerusalem [in Hebrew].

C. Van Dam, 1997, *The Urim and Thummim: A Means of Revelation in Ancient Israel*, Winona Lake IN.

J. Van Seters, 1999a, "Is There Evidence of a Dtr Redaction in the Sinai Pericope (Exodus 19-24, 32-34)?", in: L.S. Schearing and S. L. McKenzie (eds.),Those Elusive Deuteronomists: The Phenomenon of 'Pandeuteronomism' (JSOTSup. 268), Sheffield, 160–170.

J. Van Seters, 1999b, *The Pentateuch: A Social-Science Commentary*, London – New York NY.

S.M. Warner, 1980, "The Alphabet: An Innovation and its Diffusion", *VT* 30, 81–90.

M. Weinfeld, 1972, *Deuteronomy and the Deuteronomic School*, Oxford.

M. Weinfeld, 1976, "Jeremiah and the Spiritual Metamorphosis of Israel", *ZAW* 88, 17–56.

M. Weinfeld, 1978, "'They Fought from Heaven' — Divine Intervention in War in Ancient Israel and in the Ancient Near East", *EI* 14, 23–30 [in Hebrew].

M. Weinfeld, 1987, "The Traditions about Moses and Jethro at the Mount of God", *Tarbiz* 56, 449–460.

M. Weinfeld, 1990, "Traces of Hittite Cult in Shiloh and in Jerusalem", *Shnaton* 10, 107–114 [in Hebrew].

M. Weinfeld, 1992, *From Joshua to Josiah: Turning Points in the History of Israel from the Conquest of the Land Until the Fall of Judah*, Jerusalem [in Hebrew].

M. Weinfeld, "בְּרִית berith [berīṯ], covenant", *TDOT*, II, 253–279.

H. Weippert, 1972, "Die 'deuteronomistischen' Beurteilungen der Könige von Israel und Juda und das Problem der Redaktion der Königsbücher", *Biblica* 53, 301–339.

A. Weiser, *The Psalms* (transl. by H. Hartwell) (OTL), London 1962.

Z. Weisman, 1978, "The Mountain of God", *Tarbiz* 47, 107–119 [in Hebrew].

J. Wellhausen, *Prolegomena to the History of Ancient Isreal* (Eng. Transl. by J. S Black and A. Menzies), New York NY 1957 (repr.).

J. Wellhausen, *Israelitische und Jüdische Geschichte* (8th ed.), Berlin – Leipzig 1921.

R. Westbrook, 1985, "Biblical and Cuneiform Law Codes", *RB* 92, 247–264.

G. Widengren, 1970, ""What Do We Know About Moses?"", in: John I. Durham & J.R. Porter (eds.), *Proclamation and Presence; Old Testament Essays in Honour of Gwynne Henton Davies*, London, 21–47.

H.G.M. Williamson, 2011, "The Practiaclities of Prophetic Writing in Isaiah 8:1", in: *On Stone and Scroll (Fs. G.I. Davies)* (BZAW 420), Berlin, 357–369.

D.P. Wright, 2009, *Inventing God's Law: How the Covenant Code of the Bible Used and Revised the Laws of Hammurabi*, New York-Oxford.

T. Yoreh, 2003, *The Elohistic Source: Its Structure and Unity* (unpublished Dissertation; The Hebrew University), Jerusalem [in Hebrew].

T.L. Yoreh, 2010, *The First Book of God* (BZAW 402), Berlin.

Y. Zakovitch, 1982, ""A Still Small Voice"", *Tarbiz* 51, 329–346 [in Hebrew].

Y. Zakovitch, 1991, *"And You Shall Tell Your Son…": The Concept of Exodus in the Bible*, Jerusalem.

Z. Zevit, 1991, "Yahweh Worship and Worshippers in 8th-century Syria", *VT* 41, 363–366.

Z. Zevit, 2009, "Deuteronomy in the Temple: An Exercise in Historical Imagining", in: N. Sacher Fox et al. (eds.), *Mishneh Todah: Studies in Deuteronomy and Its Cultural Environment in Honor of Jeffrey H. Tigay*, Winona Lake IN, 201–218.

Index[1]

[1] Note: Page numbers followed by 'n' refer to notes.

© The Author(s), under exclusive license to Springer Nature
Switzerland AG 2024
I. Knohl, *Biblical Sinai traditions*,
https://doi.org/10.1007/978-3-031-77983-1

149

The manufacturer's authorised representative in the EU is Springer
Nature Customer Service Centre GmbH, Europaplatz 3, 69115 Heidelberg,
Germany. If you have any concerns regarding our products, please
contact ProductSafety@springernature.com

Printed and bound by CPI Group (UK) Ltd, Croydon, CR0 4YY
29/04/2026
02099545-0006